Here's what booksellers, reviewers,
and parents say about
How To Teach Your Child

"The book hits market where we don't have any similar books to offer.... Thus far, sold 7 out of the original order of 10."
—George Lucas, *Academic Aids, Inc.*
Bellevue, Washington

"We have sold seven of the nine copies ordered. It has met a need for some parents."
—Teacher Store manager
Bettendorf, Iowa

"Guides often recommend parent participation in the learning process; but how? Bautista presents a program for supplementing school teaching programs...."
—*Midwest Book Review*

"Thanks! We've been looking for a book like this."
—Carol L. Birdsong, *The Learning Center*
Waco, Texas

"I used to have difficulties in teaching my children at home to reinforce the school's teaching...But not anymore. *How To Teach Your Child* has made it easier for me! Thanks."
—Michelle Brooks
Irvine, California

"Your book is very interesting! "
—Sally Weimer
Bolingbrook, Illinois

"This manual is very specific on how to get A's in school."
—*South Florida Parenting*

"It is great for persons who need those particular items—home schoolers and parents with young children."
—Jo Miller, *Creative Schoolhouse, Inc.*
Midland, Texas

"We just started carrying this title and have sold a few, and reactions have been consistently positive from our customers."

—P.A., *Learning Path*
Gainesville, Florida

"Your book is comprehensive and easy to understand. Since I've used it to help my third-grader son with his homework, he has mastered the basics and excelled in school."

—Patricia Clemens
Greenville, Texas

"A solid resource manual."

—Diane Hathaway, *Learning Tools*
Council Bluffs, Iowa

"Well liked by parents—especially home schoolers and grandparents, buying for parents of their grandchildren."

—Lori Stanulis, *The Teacher's Pet*
Scottville, Michigan

How To Teach Your Child

THINGS TO KNOW
From Kindergarten Through Grade 6

Veltisezar B. Bautista

Bookhaus Publishers
Farmington Hills, MI 48333
U.S.A.

Library of Congress Catalog Card Number 92-71512

International Standard Book Number 0-931613-08-6

Printed in the United States of America

Address inquiries regarding rights and permissions to
Bookhaus Publishers, P.O. Box 3277
Farmington Hills, MI 48333-3277 USA

iv

Dedication

I dedicate this book to the light of my life,
Genoveva Abes-Bautista,
and to my children,
Hubert, Lester, Melvin, Ronald, and Janet,
and to all children
of parents who will read this book.

Acknowledgment

My thanks go to Claire Dionisio-Henshaw,
an elementary school teacher in the
Detroit Public Schools, for her
teaching tips, ideas, advice, and
cooperation in the preparation of this book.

Preface

Whether you're a parent who wants to teach your child at home to supplement the school's teaching, a home schooler, or a grandparent who wants to give a guidebook to the parent of your grandchildren—this book is for you!

In the early part of 1990, a reader of my book *Improve Your Grades* suggested: "Why don't you write a book for parents on how to teach their children? I've two children and want to teach them to help them learn in school, but I don't know how."

That was followed by suggestions from other parents. I then researched in libraries, browsed in bookstores, and talked with many parents to see if there were any comprehensive books on this subject. I didn't find any. Thus, I conceived the idea of writing this first comprehensive book on the subject: compact, authoritative, and easy to understand.

As a parent, I know that many parents, like you, want to teach their children at home to reinforce the school's teaching. Or perhaps you are a home schooler who wants to teach your child without any formal classroom education.

Whichever you are, here's a definitive guide that you can now use to teach your child, from writing manuscript and cursive alphabets to writing sentences and paragraphs, to knowing plants and animals and Earth and space. In the upper grades, you can let your child read some of the chapters that are self-teaching; for instance, the chapters on plants, animals, etc.

In this single volume, which you can use as a manual, you'll find the facts and guidelines you need. With this book, you'll know what your child should know at different grade levels, from kindergarten through grade 6.

Of course, school districts have their own curricula. Generally, however, due to the influence of textbooks, the curricula are organized around similar subject areas at different grade levels. Therefore, the subject areas discussed in this book are based on curricula used in the majority of public and private elementary schools throughout the country. Whatever grade your child is in, here's the only comprehensive book that guides you how to teach these subject areas to your child.

To learn the contents of the book, read one or two chapters each night. The purpose of your first reading is not to digest the subject matter, but only to get a general idea of what the book is all about. You may not want to read it from the beginning to the end; you can pick first the chapters that you like. However, I suggest that you read all the chapters in a particular unit because they are related. For example, in Unit IV—Science, you'll read chapters entitled *How Animals Live, How Plants Live, Earth and Space,* and *Physical Science.*

If you're in search of a particular term or subject matter for discussion, "photosynthesis" for instance, you may look it up in the index to find its location.

With regard to the "he/she" controversy, I would like to make this explanation: To avoid the problem, someone said I should use "he or she" or "he/she" when I refer to a child. I tried that, but I found it to be monotonous. Hence, I decided to use "he/him/his." When I say "he," I'm referring to your child, whether a boy or a girl.

As you know, a teacher usually handles a class of thirty or more students and can't teach the students one on one. Possibly not knowing that some of the students have not mastered a particular lesson due to different levels of understanding and learning, the teacher moves on to another lesson. Some of these students may go home confused and discouraged. It is at this time that a parent should help the child in solving any problem or in helping him with his lesson or homework.

However, you should discipline yourself and your child so that he can attain success in mastering the basics of every subject at home. You should teach him day in and day out, even for a short period of time—while cooking, riding in a car, or watching a baseball game. No matter how busy you are, there's always time for teaching—if you know *what* and *how* to teach.

As has been proved, the most effective way of schooling is the one-on-one teaching. With this book, you can provide this one-on-one tutoring to supplement the school's teaching or to do your own home schooling!

Veltisezar B. Bautista
Author

Table of Contents

Unit IV—Science

Unit V—Social Studies

Unit VI—Math

Unit VIII—Thinking and Study Skills

Unit I—Phonics

The Sounds of Language
18 Basic Vowel Sounds
   and 26 Consonant Sounds
Rules of Vowel and
   Consonant Sounds
How to Teach Your
   Child Phonics

1
The Sounds of Language

Many, many years ago, cave people communicated with each other by producing sounds from their mouths, moving their hands and feet, and pounding crude instruments. A man would ask, "Grrrrrwwwwwwlllll?" and the woman would reply, "Brrrrrwwwwwwlllll." Then followed their own brand of romancing and loving.

Today we humans still do the same. We produce sounds to send and receive communications, which we call *speech*. The source of sound is the airstream coming from the lungs. When we breathe, the airstream is inaudible, but when we talk, the vocal cords in the throat open and close, resulting in the breaking up of the airwaves that make the sounds.

To Communicate, Animals Make Sounds, Too

To produce different distinguishable sounds, the allies of the vocal cords—lips, tongue, palates, jaws, and cheek muscles—do their own things. But the tongue is the master of them all. In fact, it's the busiest, because it curls and pushes; it does everything possible that it can. Its tip can go from place to place, hitting the hard and soft palates or lowering or raising itself

3

with precision inside its own world. Next, the lips close and open, changing their shapes, like rapid-fire dancing in the darkness of the night. These two little, but major, parts of the human body, with jaw- and cheek-muscle movements, make specific sounds to produce speech. And to make good speech, we need to learn the correct way of saying letters, syllables, and words. Today Sean Penn may say, "I Love you," but Madonna may well reply, "I hate you!"

Alphabets

Peoples of different nations on Planet Earth learn their own alphabets to produce the sounds of their own languages.

Different Peoples, Different Languages

In the United States, parents and teachers teach children a system for mastering the alphabet, syllables, and words before studying reading, writing, and spelling in a language called American English. Educators call this system phonics.

To form a word, letters are combined and then words are lined together to form a sentence or a paragraph. At the end of sentences, we place periods, question marks, and exclamation points; at the middle, we place commas, semicolons, and colons.

The Vowels and Consonants

First, let's review all the letters in the English alphabet. They are:

Aa Bb Cc Dd Ee Ff Gg Hh Ii Jj Kk Ll Mm Nn

Oo Pp Qq Rr Ss Tt Uu Vv Ww Xx Yy Zz

The alphabet is divided into two major groups: vowels and consonants. There are only a few vowels—*a, e, i, o, u,* and sometimes *y.* All the other letters are consonants. Vowels and consonants make the sounds of language. Speech sounds in this book are indicated by letter symbols enclosed in diagonal lines (example: /r/). The diacritical marks are the breve (ă) for the short vowel; the bar or line (ā) for the long vowel; the circumflex (ô) for the simple o; and the double dot (ä) for the Italian ä.

The Vowels. Vowel sounds are produced when the airstream flows freely through the larynx and the mouth. Usually, the vowels form the core of the syllable. They can stand alone, but the consonants cannot. In other words, vowels form a partnership with consonants to create a word.

The Consonants. Consonant sounds are produced when the airstream is obstructed by the lips, the teeth, or the tongue. The busiest moments of the tongue is when it produces /l/, /t/, /d/, /r/, and /s/ sounds.

Do you know that each consonant of the alphabet may be either *unvoiced* or *voiced?*

The Unvoiced and Voiced Consonants. What's the difference between unvoiced and voiced consonants? If the vocal cords are *not vibrated,* the consonants are *unvoiced.* But you can create *voiced consonants* by sounding them through the *vibration* of the vocal cords.

The unvoiced consonant sounds are /p/, /t/, /k/, /f/, /th/ (unvoiced), /s/, /sh/, /ch/, /h/, and /wh/ (which actually sounds hw).

The voiced consonant sounds are /r/, /l/, /m/, /n/, /ng/, /y/, /w/, /b/, /d/, /g/, /th/ (voiced), /z/, and /zh/.

Of course, you already know how to pronounce words. Maybe you're even an expert at it. But maybe you produce vowel and consonant sounds differently, resulting in your speaking differently from other people. Maybe, too, you've forgotten your phonics!

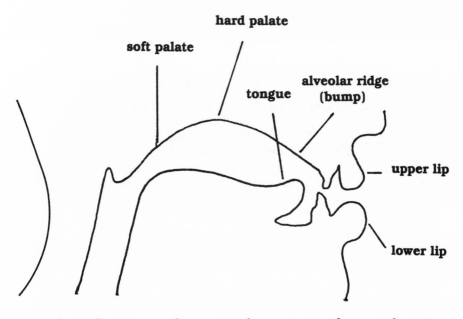

According to speech experts, there are specific procedures to follow in sounding out different vowels and consonants. Some of the hard-to-produce consonants (and how they should be pronounced) are in the following paragraphs.

1. The /l/ Sound. To sound a clear /l/, let the tip of your tongue hit the so-called "bump" (the bony alveolar ridge, which is part of the hard palate behind the upper front teeth) and then make the sound. It's harder to produce the /l/ sound when it's at the end, rather than at the beginning of a word. In making the sound of an /l/ at the end of a word, hold your tongue on the ridge as you produce the sound, such as in mall or ball. On the other hand, to make the sound of an /l/ before a final consonant, hold the tip of the tongue on the ridge, such as in milk or told.

Try it: l, l, l, l, l, l, l, l, l, l, l, l. How did you do it? Satisfied? If not, try it again.

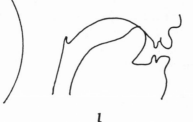

l

Practice Words:

land	fall	milk	slide
learn	mantel	old	still
legal	metal	pillow	television
look	mild	plate	wilt

2. The /r/ Sound. The /r/ sound is hard to make, especially for foreigners. Usually, a foreigner sounds r as if it were *rr*, such as in the Spanish *perro*. To produce a clear /r/, curl the tip of the tongue toward the roof of your mouth, but not touching it. Then curl the sides of the tongue to hit the inner borders of the upper molars as you make the sound.

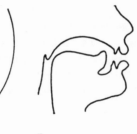

r

Try it: r, r, r, r, r, r, r, r, r, r, r, r.

Practice Words:

rag	arrange	early	narrow
ransack	car	jarred	park
ring	career	large	tour
rookie	computer	marred	verb

3. The /t/ and /d/ Sounds. You sound the /t/ by pushing the tip of your tongue onto the alveolar ridge as you discharge the air. The /t/ is clearly produced when the tongue's tip is pulled away abruptly after air is expelled *(unvoiced)*. The /d/ sound is produced the same way; however, the /d/ is clearly sounded when the tongue (not only the tip) is pulled back immediately after discharging the air. Remember, /d/ is *voiced*.

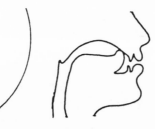

t and d

Say /t/ and /d/ alternately: t, d, t, d, t, d, t, d, t, d, t, d.

Practice Words:

/t/	talk	bat	meter
	tell	mat	state
/d/	data	induct	told
	dog	midterm	wild

4. The /s/ and /z/ Sounds. To make the /s/ sound (*unvoiced*), both lower and upper teeth should be close together, with the tongue lying flat with its tip pointing toward the alveolar ridge, but not touching it. The sides of the tongue should be inside the upper molars. Then expel the air towards the alveolar ridge.

The /z/ sound is produced the same way; however, it is *voiced.*

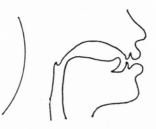

s and z

Try saying them alternately: s, z, s, z, s, z, s, z, s, z, s, z. See the difference?

Practice Words:

/s/	sing	lass	miss
	solo	master	pastel
/z/	zero	lazy	noise (**z**)
	zone	leisure (**z**)	nose (**z**)

5. The /f/ and /v/ Sounds. To produce /f/ and /v/ sounds, let your lower lip touch the upper teeth before you release the air from your mouth. Remember, /f/ is *unvoiced;* that is, the sound doesn't vibrate through the vocal cords. (The letter *f* is usually pronounced by many people as /p/ in other countries that don't have the *f* in their alphabets.)

The /v/ vibrates *(voiced).* Moreover, *v* is usually pronounced as /b/ in countries whose alphabet doesn't contain a *v.*

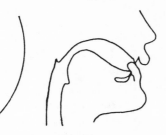

f and v

Say /f/ and /v/ alternately: f, v, f, v, f, v, f, v, f, v, f, v. Got it?

Practice Words:

/f/	fancy	afloat	influence
	fat	bluff	staff
/v/	vacation	invalid	stove
	valor	love	university

6. The /th/ Sound. The /th/ (unvoiced) sound is produced when you blow the air between the tongue tip and the upper teeth. In other words, place the tip of the tongue between the lower and upper teeth when sounding out the /th/.

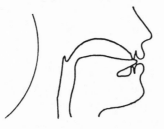

th

To make the /th/ *(voiced)* sound, place the tongue in the same position and vibrate the air between its tip and the upper teeth.

The /th/ sound is the most mispronounced consonant sound, especially by some foreigners or foreign-born citizens who have no *th* in their languages. For this reason, they pronounce /th/ (unvoiced) as /t/, and /th/ (voiced) as /d/.

Say: think (unvoiced), that (voiced), think, that, think, that, think, that, think, that, think, that.

7. The Stop Consonant Sounds. The stop consonants are /p/, /b/, /t/, /d/, /k/, and /g/. Why are they called stop consonants? Because to make these sounds, you must stop the breath or airstream and then expel it abruptly.

You produce the /p/ *(unvoiced)* and /b/ *(voiced)* sounds by holding your breath with lips closed (as if you're saying, "Read my lips!") and then discharging the air suddenly.

To produce the /k/ *(unvoiced)* sound, let the back of your tongue touch the soft palate, then abruptly release it, with the air escaping in a burst.

To make the /g/ sound, you do the same; however, the /g/ sound is *voiced.*

Did you get it? Say /p/ and /b/ and /k/ and /g/ several times: p, b, p, b, p, b, p, b, p, b, p, b; k, g, k, g, k, g, k, g, k, g, k, g.

Practice Words:

/p/	pet	slope	special
/b/	begin	blob	table
/t/	take	stat	station
/d/	door	middle	stood
/k/	kite	skate	talk
/g/	game	log	magazine

8. The Consonant Blend Sounds. Often two or more consonants are combined without any vowels between them. They are called consonant blends and are known as r-blends, l-blends, s-blends, and three-element blends. We will discuss these blends further in subsequent chapters.

Practice Words:

Unvoiced

mathematics	thin	truth
nothing	through	Smith

Voiced

bathe	lathe	then
father	rather	bother

As You Learn, You Teach

As you can see, the study of phonics is very important to a child so that he can become a good communicator. Phonics should be taught to your child as early as possible—the moment that he can sound out vowel and consonant sounds. In this way, he learns the correct pronunciation of words at an early age, which is then more likely to become a habit. "What's the point?" you may ask. The point is that if a child learns the wrong way, then he will have a hard time forgetting the old habit and remembering the new. So, as the saying goes, the earlier, the better.

But before you teach your child phonics, you should thoroughly study this chapter and the next two chapters. Throughout this book when examples are desired, you will note that they are given in parentheses immediately after the instruction.

Phonics is the very foundation of good reading, writing, and pronunciation. And remember, you don't need to be a certified phonics teacher or a Peter Jennings or a Connie Chung to teach your child phonics. By being a good student of phonics, you can be a good phonics teacher, too.

2

18 Basic Vowel Sounds and 26 Consonant Sounds

Phonics teachers and other language experts can't agree on the number of speech sounds a person can possibly make. In fact, even the dictionaries use different numbers of speech sounds and different symbols to pronounce words. Maybe they have a point. Listen to Henry Kissinger or Eva Gabor, or Jimmy Carter or Dolly Parton, talk and you'll know what I mean. Or go to Georgia, Boston, or New York and talk with some natives. You'll soon realize that they make different sounds in some words in American English.

Different Mouths, Different Sounds

Hear It on TV!

For the purpose of learning phonics, we should focus our attention on the standard English sounds as heard on radio and television newscasts. What I shall present to you is a system based on a cornucopia of major phonics systems that have been offered to the public.

The Vowel Sounds

Let's discuss the 18 basic vowel and consonant sounds.

The 18 Basic Vowel Sounds

First (Short) Sound	Second (Long) Sound	Third Sound	Additional Sounds
/ă/ ănt	/ā/ cāke	/ä/ fäther cär	/ô/—(a) tall (ar) warm (au, aw) haul lawn
/ĕ/ pĕt /ĭ/ pĭg	/ē/ jēep /ī/ bīke		/ou/—(ow) out, how
		/ô/ ôrder	/oi/—(oy) choice toy
/ŏ/ bŏx	/ō/ bōne	/oo/ (short oo) book	/er/—(ar, or) particular manor
/ŭ/ cŭp	/ū/ mūte (yoo)	/oo/ (long oo) look	(er) heater (ir) third (ur) turn (our) nourish

The vowels, as you'll learn in this chapter, are the spokesmen of the alphabet. Without them talking, the consonants can't say anything. What's the meaning of thprmpwzcyxk? Nothing! That's why the vowels, a, e, i, o, u and y must form partnerships with b, c, d, and company to create words that have meanings.

Actually, the a has five basic sounds:

1. the short /ă/, as in ănt;
2. the long /ā/, as in cāke and māke;
3. the Italian soft /ä/, as in fäther and cär;
4. the simple /ô/, as in tall—tôl, war—wôr and au and aw, (haul—hôl, and lawn—lôn); and
5. the short /ŭ/, as in alive—ŭlīv, and away—ŭwā.

Webster's dictionaries list about eight different sounds of /a/, including the so-called in-between sounds. After *qu* (sound #3), the *a* says the Italian ä as in quäd-rangle; however, the *a* after *qu* says/ô/ (sound #4) as it is *r*-controlled, as in quarter—kwôrter).

Meanwhile, the *o* has six basic sounds:
1. the short /ŏ/, as in bŏx;
2. the long /ō/, as in bōne;
3. the soft or simple /ô/, as in ôrder;
4. the short /ŭ/, as in **o**ther—**ŭ**ther and love—lŭv;
5. the short /oo/, as in b**oo**k; and
6. the long /oo/, as in l**oo**k.

However, in certain words, the *o* is not heard in the second syllable, such as in glutt**o**n.

Master these sounds. (Of course, there are other minor vowel sounds.)

Diphthongs. Diphthongs have two vowels in one syllable which, when sounded out, make one double-vowel sound. The di-phthongs are *oi* and *oy*, (f**oi**l and b**oy** which are known as the two /oi/s); *ou* and *ow* (r**ou**nd and d**ow**n, which are known as the two /ou/s); and the six *r*'s: *ar* (singul**ar**) *or* (doct**or**), *ir* (met**er**), *ir* (f**ir**st), *ur* (b**ur**n), and *our* (n**our**ish), all of which have the sound of /er/.

However, the diphthong *ou* has also the single sound of simple /ô/ such as in th**ou**ght—thôt. Meanwhile, the diphthong *ow* sometimes has the sound of a long /ō/, such as in tōw—tō and b**ow**—bō).

The Sound of /ô/ in Tall (Tôl)

On the other hand, *au, aw,* and *a* (**Saul**—**Sô**, **paw**—**pô**, and **fall-fôl**) are known as the three /au/'s. They produce the same single sound of /ô/.

But the diphthong *ar,* besides the sound of /er/ at the end of a word, has another sound—the Italian /ä/ before *r* (with the two-dotted ä in the dictionary) at the beginning or middle of a word (**ärk, cär, fär,** and **pärk**).

Other Sounds of Ou

The diphthong /ou/ also has other digraph sounds. Some examples are long /ō/ (though—thō); simple /ô/ (brought—brôt); short /ŭ/ (enoŭ**gh**—ēnŭf; short /oo/ (your—y**oo**r; long /oo/ (soup—s**oo**p); and *our,* which has the sound of /er/ (j**ou**rnal—j**er**nal). The diphthong *ur* also has the sound of /er/ (f**ur**—f**er**).

The /er/ Sound in Courteous (Certeoŭs)

Now let's go to the study of vowel digraphs, which are important parts of words.

The Vowel Digraphs. A vowel digraph is an important part of the word. It has two vowels which make one sound.

Here are samples of digraphs:

ai	*ay*	*ea*	*ee*	*ei*	*ie*
f**ai**l	s**ay**	**ea**ch	f**ee**t	c**ei**ling	p**ie**

oa	*oe*	*ou*	*ow*	*ue*	*ui*
b**oa**t	t**oe**	th**ou**gh	t**ow**	tr**ue**	s**ui**te

You must remember that in digraphs, the first vowel is pronounced long, while the second is silent.

We also have a few families of three letters that have long vowel sounds before a final blend, which are known as *special patterns*. Those words ending in *ild, ind, old, olt,* and *ost* are pronounced with long vowels. Some examples are w**ī**ld, f**ī**nd, f**ō**ld, v**ō**lt, and m**ō**st.

The Consonant Sounds

Now, let's discuss the basic consonant sounds. Again, different people have different opinions on their exact numbers.

The Basic Consonant Sounds. Even though there are varying opinions on how many basic consonant sounds there are, we will discuss the main 26 sounds.

The 26 Basic Consonant Sounds

/b/	bad	/p/	pop
c = /k/	cat	q = /kw	quick
c = /s/	center	/r/	ring
/d/	dog	s = /s/	sock
/f/	fox	s = /z/	boys
g = /g/	go	/t/	tank
g = /j/	George	/v/	van
/h/	hen	/w/	wig
/j/	jar	x = /ks/	tax
/k/	king	x = /gz/	example
/l/	lamp	x = /z/	Xerox
/m/	map	/y/	yes
/n/	neck	/z/	zoo

Other Consonant Sounds. There are other consonant sounds in our language. (See pages 22 – 24, *The Rules of Vowel and Consonant Sounds.*)

The Consonant Digraph Rule. A consonant digraph has two consonant sounds sounded together to make one sound:

ch	*sh*	*wh (hw)*	*th*
cheek	**sh**eet	**wh**o	**th**in
chain	**sh**ape	**wh**oop	clo**th**

th (voiced)	*ng*	*nk*
though	si**ng**	thi**nk**
clo**th**e	ba**ng**	ba**nk**

As you can see, the above-mentioned digraphs can be placed in front, at the middle or at the last part of a word, which are called *initial, medial,* and *final consonants.*

Many phonics teachers consider the following as consonant digraphs:

ck	*gh*	*gn*	*kn*
pa**ck**	**gh**ost	**gn**aw	**kn**ow

mn	*mb*	*ph*	*wr*
colu**mn**	la**mb**	**ph**one	**wr**ite

However, in the above-mentioned examples, one of the two letters in each digraph is silent. (According to the definition, a consonant digraph has two consonant sounds sounded together to make one sound. So I'm not sure whether the *ck, gh,* and company are really digraphs.)

The /tch/ Sound. The /tch/ sound is a consonant digraph. This spelling of the /ch/ sound is usually placed at the end of a word following a short vowel. Some examples are sti**tch**, scra**tch**, and fe**tch**.

The Consonant Blend Rule. A consonant blend has two or three consonants which are sounded out together. In other words, you can hear all the sounds of all the consonants.

Consonant Blends

/br/	**br**ing	/bl/	**bl**ack
/kr/ (cr)	**cr**eam	/kl/ (cl)	**cl**oud
/dr/	**dr**aw	/fl/	**fl**ag
/fr/	**fr**og	/gl/	**gl**ass
/gr/	**gr**ade	/pl/	**pl**ant
/pr/	**pr**actice	/sl/	**sl**ow
/tr/	**tr**ain		
/sc/ (sk)	**sk**in	/sp/	**sp**ell
/sm/	**sm**ell	/sq/	**sq**uare
/sn/	**sn**ow	/st/	**st**and

Three-Element Blends

/skr/(scr)	**scr**eam	**scr**atch
/spl/	**spl**ash	**spl**it
/spr/	**spr**ing	**spr**ay
/str/	**str**ing	**str**aight

Forget Me Not

Remember that the consonant blends, whether they are composed of two or three letters, are sounded together, and the sounds of all the consonants must be heard. For example, in saying "bring," you must not say "bering," as there should be no vowels between the two or three combined consonants.

Don't Worry,
Be Happy!

You've now learned or relearned the basic vowel and consonant sounds. Remember and practice them. After the next chapter, in which you'll learn vowel and consonant sound rules, you'll start to teach your child phonics. Don't worry, be happy! Look forward to an exciting and enjoyable time playing with words with your child!

Rules of Vowel and Consonant Sounds 3

If you go on a cross-country trip, you need a map so that you won't get lost in going to your destination. In teaching your child phonics, you need tools to guide you in your undertaking. These guides are in the forms of certain rules that help us decode words for reading, writing, and spelling.

For instance, do you know that when there are two vowels in a short word, the word may sound differently than if it has only one vowel in it? Do you know that the *s* in is and the *s* in eyes say /z/? Do you know, too, that the *s*, when added to words that end in *voiced consonants* says /z/?

Rules make it easier for us to decode words for reading, writing, or spelling. But there are some exceptions. The following paragraphs give some rules in pronounciation.

The Vowel Sound Rules

Learn the following rules for pronouncing vowels.

1. When the only vowel of a short word is at the beginning, it is usually a short sound (examples: ănt, ĕnd, ĭnk, ŭp).

2. When the only vowel of a short word is placed between two consonants, the vowel is usually pronounced short (măp, bĕg, pĭg, dŏg, bŭg). (See nonphonetic words in which /o/ is placed between two consonants and is pronounced with a short /ŭ/, instead of a short /ŏ/ (other—ŭther).

3. If there are two vowels in a short word, the first vowel is usually long and says its name, and the second is silent (māke, ēach, kīte).

4. When a word ends with the suffix *ed, er,* or *ing,* the first vowel is usually pronounced short if it is placed before two consonants (wănted, mătter, plănning).

5. When a word ends with the suffix *ed, er,* or *ing,* the first vowel is usually pronounced long if it is placed before one consonant (mēted, Pēter, wrīting).

6. When the only vowel of a short word is at the end of the word, the vowel is usually long (mā, mē, dō, gō, sō).

7. When the vowel *a* is followed by *r, l, ll,* or *lt* in the same syllable, it usually has the sound of /ô/ (war—wôr, tall—tôl, mall—môl, salt—sôlt).

8. When *y* is placed at the end of a two- or more-syllable word and is *unaccented,* it has the sound of a long /ē/ (happy—ē, lonely, puppy).

The Sound of Long /ē/ in Happy (ē)

9. When *y* is placed at the end of a two- or more-syllable word and is *accented,* it has the sound of a long /ī/ (apply—ī, imply, supply).

Almost all the rules contain the word *usually,* which means *most of the time.* In other words, there are always exceptions to the rule.

The Magic E. There are many short words with two vowels that include the *e* in the end. Usually, the first vowel is long and the *e* is silent (cāke, sīte, Pēte, mūte).

Vowels Sound Separately. Do you know that some words with two vowels sitting side by side are sounded separately? Yes, Virginia, there are vowels that are sounded separately. They do not belong to the so-called vowel digraphs (vid/e/o, di/al, and me/te/or).

The Vowel Sounds at the End or Beginning of Words. The following are general rules on vowel sounds at the end or beginning of words:

1. The *er, ir, ur,* and *our,* say /er/ (examples: **her, birth, turf, cour**tesy).

2. The *ar,* when placed at the beginning of a word or at the middle between two consonants, says the Italian /ä (**ärt, lärk, pärk**).

3. The same *ar* says /er/ in an *unaccented* syllable at the end of a word (singul**ar—er**, particul**ar**).

4. The *a* when followed by an *rr* says a short /ă/ (m**ă**rry, g**ă**rrote).

5. After *w,* the *a* in *ar* says the simple /ô/ (w**ar—wôr**, warm—w**ôrm**, w**ard—wôrd**, aw**ard—awôrd**).

6. The *o* in *or* at the beginning or at the middle (between two consonants of a word) says the simple /ô/ (**ôrder, hôrn, ôrg**anize).

7. The *or* says /er/ in an *unaccented* syllable at the end of a word (doct**or—er**, monit**or**).

8. The *or* after *w* says /er/ (*w***orst—werst**, w**ork—werk**, w**ord—werd**)

9. Generally, the letters *ium,* when at the end of a word, say an /ŭm/ sound (prem**ium—ŭm**, Val**ium**, med**ium**).

10. The letters *us* and *ous,* when placed at the end of a word, usually make the sound of /ŭs/ (cact**ŭs**, obvi**ŏŭs**, malici**ŏŭs**).

11. The *ism* in the end of a word, usually says an /iz/ŭm/ sound (bapt**ism—izŭm**, favorit**ism**, commun**ism**).

12. The *e* in the consonant *le* ending is a syllable that ends a word. In the dictionary, the last syllables in words ending in *ble, dle, ple,* and others are listed as *b'l, d'l,* and *p'l.* In other words, the *e* at the end of the syllable is silent. Naturally, the sound of the syllable is determined by the consonant at the beginning of the syllable (bub**ble**, mid**dle**, peo**ple**, bot**tle**).

13. The ending *al* says the sound of /ŭl/ (medic**al**—**ŭl**, physi-c**al**, practic**al**).

14. The ending *cle* says the sound of /kŭl/ (arti**cle**—**kŭl**, cy**cle**, cir**cle**).

15. Words ending in *ion* may have the sounds of /ŭn, /yŭn/, /jŭn/, or /eŭn/ (fash**ion** , medall**ion**, reg**ion**, champ**ion**).

16. The ending *ian* says the sound of /eŭn/ (beautic**ian**—**eŭn**, music**ian**, Iran**ian**).

17. The ending *ture* says the /chĕr/ sound (pas**ture**—**cher**, pic-**ture**, tor**ture**).

18. In some words, the *tu* at the middle of a word says /chĕ/ (congra**tu**late—congra**chĕ**late, na**tu**ral, cul**tu**ral).

The Simple O, Short O, or What? When the *o* is placed between two consonants at the beginning of a word, it's really confusing. You don't know whether to pronounce it as a short /ŏ/, a simple /ô/, or a long /ō/ (c**o**mplex, c**o**ntour, c**o**mb, c**o**lumn, c**o**mmand, g**o**vernment, m**o**del, c**o**mix).

If you're not sure how to pronounce it (teach this to your child, also), make the /o/ sound like an /ĕ/. In that way, your pronunciation is in between.

The Consonant Sound Rules

Since we've discussed the vowel sound rules, let's now learn the consonant sound rules. Here we go!

The Sounds of C, X, and Q. The letters *c*, *x*, and *q* have no sounds of their own, like the singers in the Milli Vanilli singing group who lypsynched other singers. The consonant *c* can be hard or soft. C sounds like /k/ when it is placed before vowels *a*, *o*, and *u* (**c**at, **c**ot, **c**ut) and when placed before a consonant (**c**limate). It sounds like /s/ when placed before *e*, *i*, and *y* (**c**ent, pre**c**inct, **c**ycle). The letter *q* sounds like /kw/ (**q**uick—**kw**uick, **q**uack, **q**uarter).

The Tri-X. The consonant x represents three sounds: /ks/, /gz/, and /z/. When placed at the end of a word, *x* sounds like /ks/ (ta**x**); at the end of the syllable *ex*, it may sound like /gz/ or /ks/ (**ex**it—**egz**it, te**xt**—te**ks**); and at the beginning of a word, *x* sounds like /z/ (**x**ylophone).

Go, George, Go! The consonant *g* has two sounds: hard and soft. The letter *g* says /g/ when placed before vowels *a*, *o*, and *u* (**g**ame, **g**one, **g**un).   The soft *g* becomes *ge* and says /j/ at the end of a word (bad**ge**—bad**j**, led**ge**, nud**ge**). The letter *g* says /j/ before *e, i,* and *y* (**ge**ometry—**je**ometry, **gi**ant, **gy**m), with some exceptions (**ge**t, **gi**ve, **gi**rl). Moreover, the three letters *age* sound like /ĭj/ at ends of words (vill**age**—**ĭj**, cabb**age**, lugg**age**).

The S or Z? Sometimes, the ending *se* sounds like a /z/ when placed at the end of a word (no**se**—nō**z**). The sound /s/ is made after voiceless letters *t, p, k,* and *f* in plural forms (mat**s**, map**s**, bank**s**, staff**s**). However, the *s* sounds like a /z/ when used in plurals after *voiced* consonants (thug**s**—**z**, letter**s**, wall**s**, (See Voiced Consonants on page 5.)

The Sound of z as in Nose—Nōz

We add *es,* instead of *s,* in words ending in *s* (bas**es**), *x* *(tax**es**),* *z (buzz**es**), ch* (switch**es**), and *sh* (slash**es**) to form the plural forms.

The Past Tense. The ending letters *ed* have three sounds.

1. They sound like /ĕd/ when placed after *t* and *d* to form a past tense (examples: rest**ed**, bend**ed**, rent**ed**).

2. They sound like a /t/ after *ch (*pin**ch**ed—**t**), *sh* (slas**h**ed), *ck* (che**ck**ed), *f* (puf**f**ed, *k* (li**k**ed), *p* (tri**pp**ed), *s* (mis**s**ed), and *x* (mi**x**ed).

3. They sound like a /d/ after any other sounds (dragge**d**, kille**d**, ruine**d**, penne**d**).

Other Consonants with Different Sounds. There are some consonants which convey other sounds. They are *ph, gh, ch,* and *sh.*

1. *Letters ph and gh.* The consonants *ph* and *gh* are both pronounced as /f/ (**ph**armacy, rou**gh**, enou**gh**). However, *gh* is sometimes pronounced as a hard /g/ (**gh**etto and a silent *gh* (li**gh**t).

The Sound of /f/ in /gh/ (Enough!)

2. *The Three Faces of Ch.* The *ch* represents three sounds: /ch/ (**ch**eek), /sh/ (**Ch**icago), and /k/ (**ch**emistry).

3. *Other Duties of Ch and Sh.* The letters /ch/ and /sh/ also play important roles in the ends of words. The sound /chĕr/ represents *ture* (adven**ture**—**chĕr**). The /sh/ stands for *tion* (vaca**tion**—**shŭn**), *sion* (admis**sion**—**shŭn**), and *ci* (mali**ci**ous—**shŭs**), *ti* (pala**ti**al—**shŭl**), and *sure* (as**sure**—**shĕr**). But in some words, **zhĕr** represents *sure* (plea**sure**—**zhĕr**, trea**sure**, mea**sure**). On the other hand, /sh/ also represents /ch/ in some other words (ma**ch**ine, Mi**ch**igan, **Ch**evrolet).

4. *Some Additional Sounds.* Many words ending in *si, zi,* and *zure* have the sounds of /z/ (televi**si**on—**zhŭn**), glazier—**zhĕr**), sei**zure**—**zhĕr**).

The Silent Letters. There are also consonants which are not pronounced. In other words, they are included in a word, but they are silent.

Silent Letters	Combinations	Examples
b	mb	lam**b**
	bt	de**b**t
c	ck	pi**c**k
	sc (followed by e or i)	**sc**issor
d	dg	le**d**ge
g	gn	si**g**n
h	rh	**h**onor, r**h**inoceros
k	kn	**k**now
l	lf	ha**l**f
	lk	wa**l**k
	lm	pa**l**m
n	mn	colum**n**
p	pn	**p**neumonia
	ps	**p**sychiatry
s	sl	ai**s**le
	st	li**s**ten
t	tch	sti**t**ch
	tle	whis**t**le
w	wr	**w**rong
	sw	ans**w**er

Prefixes, Root Words, and Suffixes

A syllable or letters added at the beginning or end of a word give different meanings. The following are some examples of prefixes, root words, and suffixes:

Prefix	Meaning	Sample Word
ab	away from	**ab**sent
pre	before	**pre**cede

Root	Meaning	Sample Word
annu	year	**annu**ally
bio	life	**bio**graphy

Suffix	Meaning	Sample Word
ac	like	mani**ac**

Rules for Syllabication

Because syllabication is an important aid in writing and pronouncing words, it is included in phonics. As the word indicates, syllabication is the process of dividing words into syllables. For this reason, we have to remember some rules pertaining to syllabication.

1. A short word consisting of only one vowel sound is not divided (examples: map, chalk, face).

2. A compound word consisting of two simple words is divided between the twin words (base/ball, on/to, rain/bow).

3. A word with a prefix is divided between the prefix and the root (**un**/tapped, **in**/hale, **trans**/port).

4. A word with a suffix is divided between the root and the suffix (nice/**ly**, read/**ing**, small/**ness**).

5. A vowel sounded alone in a word makes a syllable by itself (**a**/mass, **o**/range, mon/**i**/tor).

6. A word that has two vowels that are sounded separately is divided between the twin vowels (vid/**e**/**o**, di/**al**, ra/di/**o**).

7. A word with one consonant between two vowels is usually divided after the first vowel, if the vowel is pronounced long (nā/tion, pā/per, pā/tient).

8. A word that has one consonant between two vowels is usually divided after the consonant if the first vowel is pronounced short (pĕr/ish, păl/ace, lăv/ish).

9. A word that has two or more consonants between two vowels is usually divided between the first two consonants (mat/ter, bot/tle, for/tune). Exceptions: Blends and strong consonant digraphs (*sh, ch, ck, wh,* and *th*) are not separated (back/er, march/es, quick/en, breath/less).

10. A word that ends in *le* following a consonant is usually divided before the consonant (Bi/ble, tri/ple, min/gle). Exception: The digraph *ck* is not divided (tack/le, buck/le, nick/le).

Now Is the Time!

Since you now know the many rules in phonics and how to make the correct sounds of words, you can supplement the school's teaching of phonics to your child.

How to Teach Your Child Phonics

4

Teaching phonics to children is not the certified teacher's monopoly. You, too, as a parent, can teach phonics to your child after you've studied its rudiments and fundamentals. If you've forgotten your phonics or you haven't studied it at all before, you can teach it to your child as soon as you master the contents of the first three chapters of this book. The important thing to remember is that as you study, you learn, and as you learn, you transmit your knowledge to your child. That's teaching.

The best period to teach your child is when he is in kindergarten. For a whole year before he enters the first grade, you can teach him phonics so that he'll have a good foundation in reading, writing, and spelling. Of course, you can teach phonics at whatever age he is.

Spoken Words into Visual Words

The first thing is to teach the letters of the alphabet. Emphasize to your child that to translate spoken words into visual words, you must combine written symbols composed of different letters. These symbols are vowels and consonants.

The Art of Writing

Of course, before you can teach your child phonics, you have to teach him to write the letter symbols in manuscript (print) and cursive forms. Usually, manuscript is taught in the first and second grades, and cursive writing in the third and fourth grades. But some schools go straight to teaching cursive forms, thereby eliminating writing in manuscript. But it seems that the manuscript style should be first learned by children, because they normally see printed letters in reading materials, including books.

Show to your child the correct way to write the manuscript and cursive alphabets, with the 1-2-3 steps as indicated with numbers and arrows on the next pages. The numbers show the sequence of strokes while the arrows show the direction of strokes.

Manuscript Alphabet

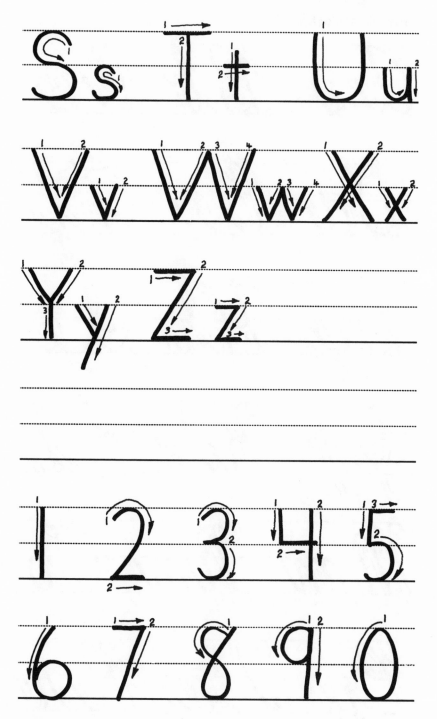

Cursive Alphabet

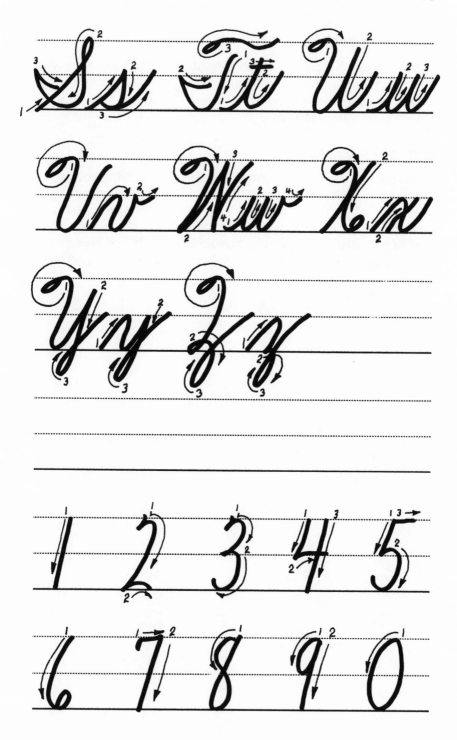

What's Next?

After your child has learned to write the letter symbols, you must explain to him the definition of a vowel, a consonant, a digraph, and other terms. In that way, he'll understand what you're trying to teach him.

The Way to Do It

Here's a guideline that you may follow in teaching your child (or you can make your own outline, as long as you cover all the basic fundamentals of phonics). You can always refer to chapters 1 through 3 when you cover the following subjects. However, if phonics is taught in school, then you should coordinate your work with the teacher's schedule of phonics instructions.

Guideline for Instructions

I. Introduction
- A. Learning the alphabet
- B. Basic vowel sounds
- C. Unvoiced and voiced consonants
- D. Diphthongs
- E. Vowel digraphs
- F. Basic consonant sounds
- G. Other consonant sounds
- H. Consonant digraphs
- I. Consonant blends

II. Vowel and consonant sound rules
- A. Vowel sounds
- B. Consonant sounds
  1. The sounds of *c, x,* and *q, s* and *z*
  2. The silent letters

III. Short vowel sounds
- A. Short vowels (*a, e, i, o, u,* and sometimes *y)*
- B. Two-syllable words (simple endings)

IV. Long vowel words
- A. Long vowel patterns
  1. Short syllable words pronounced long (nō, gō)
  2. The magic *e* (short syllables or words that end in *e* are usually sounded long)
  3. Long vowel partners (*ai, ay; ee, ea; oa, ow;* and *ou, ui*)
  4. More long vowel partners (*ew, eu; ei, ey;* and *ie, ou.*)
- B. Other vowel partners
  1. ea
  2. ou (short /oo/)
  3. ou (short /ŭ/)
  4. ui (short /ĭ/)
- C. Short and long /oo/
  1. short /oo/
  2. long /oo/
- D. Word endings (*le, us, ous,* and *ium)*
- E. Prefixes, roots, and suffixes (*ab* and *pre, annu* and *bio, ac,* and *ment)*

In teaching your child phonics, you first teach him the one-vowel words, such as boy, pen, and log; then the two-vowel words, such as notebook, number, and happy.

In introducing the sounds of vowels, emphasize that the *a* has five major sounds:

1. the short /ă/ (**ă**ct);
2. the long /ā/ (t**ā**ke);
3. the Italian /ä/ (f**ä**ther);
4. the *a*, which sounds a simple /ô/ in words with *a* before *l* or *ll* or *r* t**a**lk—tôk, sm**a**ll—smôl, w**a**rm—wôrm); the *a* in *au* and *aw* words (m**au**l—môl, p**aw**—pô); and

5. the short /ŭ/ in words (**a**live—**ŭ**līv, **a**way—**ŭ**wā, **a**round—**ŭ**round).

The ô Sound in (Maul—Môl)

In the lower grades, you can first teach the short and long /a/'s; then in the upper grades, you can show the other sounds of /a/. In other times, teaching depends on the ability of the child to learn what he's studying. If he's a slow learner, then be slow; if he's a fast learner, then be faster in giving instructions.

The vowels with r's are very important since *a, e, i, o,* and *u* are combined with *r* or *rr* in many words. Just remember that *er, ir, ur,* and *our* are known as the four /er's/; that is, words with these letters (met**er**, b**ir**th, b**ur**n, j**our**ney) have the same /er/ sounds. The *ar* and *or,* when placed at the middle or end of a word, also have the sound of /er/. However, the *a* in *ar,* when placed at the beginning or middle of a word, says the Italian /ä/ (**ä**rk, m**ä**rk, d**ä**rk).

The above-mentioned word endings should be taught in the upper elementary grades. However, if your child in the lower grades can tackle them, so much the better.

Patience is very important in teaching phonics to the young student. You can't expect him to instantly acquire the knowledge of the sounds of vowels and consonants in a very short time. Even as an adult, if you study a foreign language, you have to first study the alphabet; then the sounds of vowels and consonants; and then the combinations of vowels and consonants. Just remember, too, that English is not a perfect phonetic language; that is, a language in which words are pronounced just as they are spelled.

But, generally, if your child knows phonics, he'll have the edge in decoding words to aid him in reading, writing, and spelling.

Why Johnny Can't Read

In his book *Why Johnny Can't Read*, Robert Flesch gives some commonly misspelled words which can be avoided if one is proficient in phonics. Below is an excerpt from the book. (Reprinted from *Why Johnny Can't Read* by Rudolf Flesch. Copyright © 1955 and 1983 by Rudolf Flesch. Used by permission of Harper Collins Publishers, Inc. New York, NY.)

> There are, for instance, the common misspellings "writting," "occasion," and "suceed." The reason for "writting" is of course that *written* has two *t*'s and so the poor speller has a dim notion that there are also two *t*'s in *writing*. *Occasion*, he knows, has two *c* or *s*'s. But which? He guesses, and nine times out of ten he guesses wrong. As to *succeed*, he has a feeling that there *can't* be a double *c* in English; isn't it always *ck*? So he writes "suceed."
>
> A person trained in phonics can't possibly make any of these mistakes. He *knows*. He knows that a double consonant results in a short vowel sound and that therefore "writting" would rhyme with sitting. He knows that the *zh* sound in *occasion* can only be spelled with a single *s* and that *ocassion* would rhyme with *fashion;* he knows that the sound *ks* as in *succeed* is sometimes spelled *cc* as in *accent, flaccid,* and *accident.*

As you can see in the above quotation, knowledge of phonics helps students in decoding words for writing, spelling, and pronunciation.

The Way to Teach

Be sure that, as you teach your child to read, write, and spell, you give him examples of words, using each in a sentence. Later, you let him give examples of his own. In that way, he'll remember what he has studied and learned as your lessons progress.

Generally, young children find it hard to pronounce /r/ and /th/. Let your child control the /r/, not the other way around. As you know, the /th/ is pronounced unvoiced (thin) and voiced (there).

In introducing the prefixes, root words, and suffixes, teach the student that when syllables are added to the beginning or end of a word, such additions change the word's meaning (loved, **un**loved; regular, **ir**regular) or may give an additional meaning.

As a parent, you can teach your child phonics. Just remember, a child can learn any language at a young age, even as early as three, in whatever environment he's in (if he's an American or whatever and is raised in Russia, he'll learn Russian; if in China, Chinese; and if in Baghdad, Iraqi).

Happy teaching!

Unit II—Reading

How to Raise a Good Reader

Teaching Vocabulary

Make Your Child
  a Good Speller

Perceptual Skills
  and Word Analysis

Reading Comprehension

How to Raise a Good Reader   5

Reading is one of the basic subjects that every pupil anywhere in the world needs in his everyday life to be proficient in any other school subjects. By and large, if he's already a good reader, he understands instructions, knows what to do, and learns the gist of whatever he reads.

Whatever his rate of development, your child can benefit from his exposure to language. At first, he listens to you, then he imitates what you say. After you teach him to read and write, he reads through your guidance. Therefore, as a parent and your child's first teacher, you play an important part in his improvement of skills in listening, speaking, writing, and reading.

The Rules of the Game

If you want to make your child a good reader, you must make reading guidelines and create an environment conducive to reading and learning at home.

Of course, a baby can't be taught to read at a very early age. At birth, the baby cries aloud as if saying, "I've arrived! Come and hug me!" That's his first communication with you. At that time, of course, you won't teach reading. In the first weeks and months, you continually communicate with your baby in a gentle voice. You talk, he listens. Even if he doesn't know yet what you're talking about, you let him "read your lips." He hears your voice as you ask, "How are you?" "So you just woke up?" "Would you like to sleep again?" "Would you like to eat now?" and so on and on. Of course, you're not crazy; you just naturally do it.

Word Games

If you want your child to be a successful reader, play word games with him. Actually, a *word game* is a *word drill*. Its name has been changed so that it may connote fun; thus, your child will enjoy what he's doing.

Generally, a word game involves cards with words that name things or describe actions. But it may also involve other things, such as the cutting out by your child of big words and pictures from newspapers and magazines; then, he may paste the words under the appropriate pictures on pieces of bond paper. Of course, in these games your child has the chance to win, lose or draw.

Word games can be purchased in stores, particularly in school supply and teachers' stores. But you can make your own word games made of cards with words; for instance, cards with words that sound alike or look alike. Or you can ask his teacher what word games are played in school. In fact, some schools send out booklets on how to make and play some word games.

Hi! How are you?

Tips from the Experts

Here are some tips from reading experts on how to raise your child to be a good reader:

■ Start reading aloud to him as soon as he's able to sit in your lap. Although he may not understand the words you're saying, he'll think that reading is for pleasure and learning. He'll learn that letter symbols have meaning and that books are full of information or interesting stories.

■ Be the role model. Set the example by reading a lot at home. By seeing you as an avid reader, he'll become one, too. If possible, have a set of encyclopedia in a study room or a small library, where a lot of good books and magazines can be found. Naturally, picture books are very good tools for young children.

■ Buy books that interest him. If he's a sports fan, buy books about baseball, football, or hockey and the great athletes who play those games. If he's a fan of Vanna White, then let him have a book about Vanna, if there is one, or the book *Vanna Speaks* by Vanna herself. If he likes animals, then, by all means, acquire books about animals. If he likes war machines and equipment, buy him books about the Stealth bombers, Tomahawk missiles, or other war weapons. In summary, whatever your child is interested in, buy books on those subjects.

■ Keep reading to him until he can read by himself. If reading becomes a habit, he'll grow up as a good reader. Remember that statistics show that children who are read to by adults at home develop a love for books and excel in reading.

■ Especially during the weekend, take him to the library and let him select his own books for reading. In other words, make the local library his second school.

Techniques of Reading

Particularly in the upper grades, your child must be taught the techniques of reading. These techniques may be divided into *previewing, skimming, scanning,* and *digesting.*

Previewing. *Previewing* is like overviewing or surveying. If you go to see a movie, *How The Gulf War Was Won* for instance, you'll see previews of coming attractions. In this way, you are given the idea of what the coming pictures are all about.

In previewing a book, a student must read the title, the subtitle, the author's name, the table of contents, the boldfaced headings, the subheadings, the introduction, the afterword, the appendix, the index, and some of the maps, graphs, charts, and illustrations.

While previewing doesn't give all the details, it does keep you from spending your time on things that the author wrote, but that you don't want to read.

Previewing Is Like Overviewing

Skimming. *Skimming* is reading quickly and lightly, searching for factual information that will lead to answers to the questions of *who? what? where?* and *when?* (Who were those people involved? What really happened? Where did it happen? When did it happen?) When you teach your child skimming, let him search for one or two keywords in each paragraph that will answer the questions that you want to have answered.

Scanning. *Scanning* is a quick, orderly lookout for keywords or phrases that will answer the questions of *who? what? where? when? how?* and *why?* with emphasis on the last two. Scanning, however, will be slower than skimming because you are looking for specific facts. Furthermore, teach your son or daughter to look at subheadings, words and phrases printed in **bold** type or *italics*, and one or two keywords in each paragraph. Remember, scanning gives you more information than skimming. In scanning, let him interpret ideas and thoughts that create relationships between things, facts, or events. In doing so, he must also predict relationships while, at the same time, look for the answers to the questions.

Digesting. This is the slowest type of reading. One must grasp ideas and thoughts, do analytical thinking, and interpret the hows and whys, in addition to answering the who? what? where? and when? questions. Your pupil must read thoroughly enough to be able to evaluate, describe, or interpret places, facts, or events. In this type of reading, develop in your child the skills to gather and sort facts and ideas for importance and relationships, and to later evaluate those facts and ideas.

Tips on Reading Skills

Here are some tips on how you can help your child enhance his comprehension skills:

1. When reading a story, ask him to think of questions about the title or some illustrations in the book. This may lead to his motivation to read the story.

2. Ask him to summarize what he has read.

3. In watching a TV soap opera, help him to predict as to what will happen next.

4. Always ask the question *why?* when something occurs in a story. That encourages active thinking.

5. Ask him about several events that happened during the day. That can help him develop skills in sequencing.

Things to Remember

If you buy some reading materials from learning center stores and teachers' stores where you can also purchase some teaching aids, so much the better. For the primary grades, you acquire storybooks with large type and many attractive illustrations.

Have Books, Will Read

Needless to say, if you expose your child to books and other reading materials and develop in him the above skills, there's no doubt that he will become a lover of books and a good reader. And good readers usually excel in school.

Teaching Vocabulary 6

Before you enroll your child in kindergarten, teach him some vocabulary words. At first, teach the parts of the body: head, face, nose, and so on. Next, teach him the words of some objects in the house and parts of the house itself. Afterwards, show and name the objects outside the home. Then buy some reading blocks and picture books showing objects and some actions.

Let Your Child Play with Toys and Words

Subject Areas

★ ★ ★ ★ ★

Kindergarten

As a pupil in kindergarten, your child must already show an interest in words and symbols and recognize his own name in print. At this time, teach him manuscript handwriting (printing) and how to write his own name and address. (For manuscript writing, see pages 30–31.)

At the same time, teach him the upper-case and lower-case letters and the combinations of upper-case and lower-case letters, such as names of persons, things, and places.

Examples of proper nouns that should be capitalized are Catherine, Wednesday, Iraq, Jordan, and Iran. Every sentence should begin in capital letters. Example: "He is going to war."

Symbols Represent Words

Explain to him that printed words represent spoken words. Give vocabulary words that he can understand and remember—that is, words that convey simple ideas that he can easily grasp.

★ ★ ★ ★ ★

Grade 1

A, B, C, and Company

By this time, he must memorize the letters of the alphabet in sequence. Continue teaching him how upper-case and lower-case letters are combined to give different meanings. In other words, teach which beginnings of words are capitalized and which aren't. (See *Rules on Capitalization* on page 102.)

★ ★ ★ ★ ★

Grade 2

Homonyms, Synonyms, and Antonyms

At this grade level, start teaching
- *homonyms*, words that sound the same, but with different meanings;

- *synonyms*, words with the same meanings; and
- *antonyms*, words with opposite meanings.

These three *nyms* continue to grow as part of the English language. In fact, the word *madman* may have another meaning in the dictionary, but it can also mean Saddam.

Sample Words

Homonyms	Synonyms	Antonyms
to, too, two	pretty, beautiful	weak—strong
were, where	rot, decay	soft—hard
meet, meat	shift, switch	smooth—rough
air, heir	surround, encircle	lazy—industrious

Likewise, proceed teaching simple vocabulary words, such as those with single and double syllables.

Samples of One-Syllable Words

cart	top	pipe
mat	pet	ears
boy	girl	face
born	burn	rope
toy	mouse	shirt

Samples of Two-Syllable Words

mo/tel	hur/ry	i/cy
ri ot	pi lot	bo nus
re cent	dust y	cen sus
cop y	jel ly	pen cil
ba by	zip per	sup ply
pho to	wom an	mar ry

★ ★ ★ ★ ★

Grade 3

To Israel or to Saudi Arabia?

At this grade level, your child should be expected to know the meaning and use of direction words, color words, curriculum words, action words, and function words.

Examples of direction words are:
1. Write the word *school* on the side of the bus.
2. Draw a boy with black hair sitting on the chair.
3. Color the chair brown.

Also, your child must not only know single- and double-syllable words, but also some three-syllable words.

Samples of Three-Syllable Words

cov/er/age	won/der/ful	u/ni/fy
nom i nate	gas o line	dec o rate
u ni form	mi cro phone	du ra tion
oc ca sion	im por tant	mon u ment
peace ful ly	pro fes sion	con fu sion

In the lower grades, teach your child sight words that can be recognized instantly.

★ ★ ★ ★ ★

Grades 4, 5, and 6

In the upper elementary grades, the student must be given longer and more complicated words. You may now include four- five-, and six-syllable words.

Samples of Four-Syllable Words

ac/cu/mu/late	con/fi/den/tial	sub/stan/tial
ex on er ate	in vest ti gate	re frig er ate
com men ta ry	hon or ar y	com mu ni ty
o rig i nal	cem e ter y	ad ver sa ry
e lec tri cian	par a liz ing	tem per a ture

Samples of Five-Syllable Words

math/e/ma/ti/cian	sup/ple/men/ta/ry	i/mag/i/na/ble
com pre hen sive ly	com mu ni ca ble	ex plan a to ry
sat is fac to ry	i mag i na tive	u ni lat er al
in con se quen tial	un nec es sa ry	re de vel op ment

Sight Words

You start giving sight words to your child even in preschool or kindergarten. These sight words, also known as learned words, must be memorized.

220 Dolch Basic Sight Word List

Kindergarten

a	jump	we	get	say
and	little	where	good	she
away	look	yellow	have	so
big	make	you	he	soon
blue	me	all	into	that
can	my	am	like	there
come	not	are	must	they
down	one	at	new	this
find	play	ate	no	too
for	red	be	now	under
funny	run	black	on	want
go	said	brown	our	was
help	sea	but	out	well
here	the	came	please	went
I	three	did	pretty	what
in	to	ran	white	who
is	two	eat	ride	will
it	up	four	saw	with
				yes

Grade I

after	every	him	of	stop
again	fly	his	old	take
an	from	how	once	thank
any	give	just	open	them
as	going	know	over	then
ask	had	let	put	than
by	has	live	round	think
could	her	may	some	walk
				were

Grade II

always	cold	green	sing	use
around	does	its	sit	very
because	don't	made	sleep	wash
been	fast	many	tell	which
before	first	off	their	why
best	five	or	these	wish
both	found	pull	those	work
buy	gave	read	upon	would
call	goes	right	us	write
				your

Grade III

about	drink	hot	much	show
better	eight	hurt	myself	six
bring	fall	if	never	start
carry	far	keep	only	ten
clean	full	kind	own	today
cut	got	laugh	pick	together
done	grow	light	seven	try
draw	hold	long	shall	warn

Dolch Sight Phrases

(Made from the Ninety-five Most Common Nouns and the Basic Sight Vocabulary)

from home	I was
I will go	too little
the little children	my father
will look	a new book
you are	by the tree
all night	as I do
her father	the yellow cat
the red apple	has come
in the garden	he is
what I say	down there
the little chickens	your sister
will think	if you wish

you were
all day
her mother
the red cow
about him
as he said
did not fall
can play
it is
with mother
has found
for the girl
then he came
the little dog
went down
I am
too soon
my brother
a pretty picture
for the baby
I may get
the little pig
is coming

you will do
down the hill
did not go
for him
at home
the white duck
would like
if I must
I will come
to the nest
will go
for them
at school
the white sheep
would want
if I may
then he said
in the water
must go
on the floor
so much
the new coat

The above list contains sight words and phrases used by majority of elementary schools in this country.

Ways to Improve Vocabulary

Here are some ways to improve your child's vocabulary:

1. Let him read, read, read. Let him be a "wide-reader." Get him into the habit of reading books, newspapers, coupons, and even junk mail that says, "You've already won a free trip to Baghdad!"

Read, Read, Read

2. Let a dictionary and a thesaurus be his best friends. Show him how to look up words in them. Sometimes, words create new meanings. For instance, the word *patriot* has now a new meaning in the dictionary as an antimissile missile (spelled with a capital P) because of the war in the Persian Gulf.

3. Give him a list of at least ten vocabulary words a day and let him list at least the same number of words, knowing the meaning of each word and how to use it. Year by year, dictionary words increase in numbers. The word *Scud,* for instance, is now to be recognized by the dictionary as a missile.

4. Teach him how to solve crossword puzzles. These brain twisters will force him to learn new words.

5. Teach him prefixes, suffixes, and roots. Most words are made up of small parts, so try to have him identify an individual part or parts of a word to gain access to its meaning. Many of the roots, prefixes, and suffixes come from native English (Anglo-Saxon), Latin, and Greek word stems.

Study Prefixes, Suffixes, and Roots of Words

Native English Prefixes and Roots

Prefix	Meaning	Root	Example
fore	ahead, before	cast	**fore**cast
mis	not correct	lead	**mis**lead
under	below	estimate	**under**estimate
a	in, on, at	wake	**a**wake
in	in, into	doors	**in**doors
out	outside, beyond	distance	**out**distance
un	not	sure	**un**sure

Native English Suffixes and Roots

Suffix	Meaning	Root	Example
ly	like when, how	kind	kind**ly**
		week	week**ly**
er	one who, that which	box	box**er**
hood	state of	nation	nation**hood**
less	without, lacking	shoe	shoe**less**
some	inclined to	hand	hand**some**

Latin Prefixes

Prefix	Meaning	Example
ab	away from	**ab**sent
ad	to, forward	**ad**vance
de	away from	**de**part
dis	apart, opposite of	**dis**assemble
in, im,	not	**in**appropriate
		improper
ir, il)		**ir**regular
		illegitimate
pre	before	**pre**cede
re	again, back	**re**turn
sub	under, below	**sub**marine

Latin Suffixes

Suffix	Meaning	Example
an, ian	one who	Iran**ian**
ment	act of	entertain**ment**

ive	of, relating to	objec**tive**
ic	like, having to do with	ton**ic**
ary, ory	relating to	diction**ary** crema**tory**

Latin Roots

Root	Meaning	Example
dict	tell	pre**dict**
mit	send	trans**mit**
script	write	tran**script**
vers, vert	turn	re**verse**, di**vert**
voke	call	pro**voke**

Greek Stems or Word Parts

Word Part	Meaning	Example
auto	self	**auto**matic
bio	life	**bio**graphy
micro	small	**micro**scope
phone	sound	micro**phone**
tele	far off	**tele**phone
thermo	heat	**thermo**stat
meter	measurement	speedo**meter**

These are only a few of the many native roots, prefixes, and suffixes from native English, Latin, and Greek words.

In analyzing words, coach your child to use these word stems and other prefixes and suffixes. As you know, you can divide words into different parts to learn their meaning. The secret is in knowing keywords. For example, when we analyze the word *anthropology,* if we know that *anthropo-* means man and *logy* means study, we can see that anthropology means *the study of man.*

The dictionaries contain hundreds of roots, prefixes, and suffixes. If your child memorizes many of them and learns their meanings, he'll be able to understand thousands of words, even including those that he may see for the first time.

Teach him the value of looking up in the dictionary every word appropriate for his grade level. Let him acquire the habit of listing about ten words every day to be memorized and remembered. That will be 300 words a month and 3,650 words a year.

Dictionary Skills

In looking up words in the dictionary, teach him dictionary skills—that is, how to look up words in A-B-C order. For example, show him how to group words such as the following in A-B-C order: table, chair, flower (which should be grouped as chair, flower, table).

Let him know that if the words have the same beginning letters, he must look at the second letters. Example: big, bad, beg (which should be grouped as bag, beg, big). If the first two letters of a word are the same, tell him to look at the third letter of each word to be put in A-B-C order, such as Saddam, salami, Saturn. Let him use the same procedure in words with the same first three letters, and so on.

Know Your Child's True Friends

The dictionary and the thesaurus are two of the best friends that can help him improve his vocabulary in the elementary grades, high school, and even college.

Make Your Child a Good Speller   7

If you want your child to be a good speller, act now. For as you know, at an early age and before going to school, every child should be taught by his parents to read and spell. Thus, his interest and ability in spelling depend largely on what or how you and his teachers teach him.

When your child reads a lot, he sees many words, and when he sees them, he remembers how they are spelled. As one of my journalism professors said, "To be a good newspaperman, you must read, read, read, and write, write, write." To be a good speller, the same advice holds true.

When your child is in kindergarten or primary grades, make it a habit, when you're with him on the way to school or shopping, to let him read road or building signs. In that way, he'll learn the spelling of words. Of course, not all signs are spelled correctly, and you must give the correct spelling.

In stores, let him read labels on items written in big letters; on T-shirts painted with slogans, such as, *My brother went to the desert and all that's left of him is this lousy T-shirt;* and on book titles, such as *How Scuds Terrorized Israelis and How They Didn't Retaliate* by CNN reporters. These are just examples.

Memorization Time

At whatever grade level your child is, give him a list of spelling words to be memorized every day. Persuade him to copy each list in a separate notebook for vocabulary and spelling.

Notebook for Vocabulary and Spelling

In the lower grades (kindergarten and primary grades), teach your child that the /k/ sound is spelled *k* in some words and *ck* in other words. Here are two general rules:

1. Spelled k. The /k/ sound is spelled *k* after a consonant (mi**lk**), after a long vowel sound (bīke), and after two vowels (st**ea**k).

Sample Words

dūke	shāke	smoke
snāke	chōke	cōke
croak	lāke	māke
cook	brook	crook

2. Spelled ck. The /k/ sound is spelled *ck* at the end of a syllable or a word directly after a single short vowel (p**ĭck**, st**ĭck**, r**ăck**).

Sample Words

cl**ŏck**	c**ŏck**	ch**ĕck**
st**ŏck**	sm**ŏck**	cr**ŏck**
d**ŭck**	s**ŏck**	p**ăck**
p**ŏck**et	kn**ŏck**	w**ĭck**

Also, let him realize that suffixes such as *er, en, et, y,* and *ed* can be added to words ending in *k* and *ck.* Some examples are ba**cker**, bla**cken**, po**cket**, smo**ky**, and ki**cked**. Your child can memorize difficult words which cannot be decoded based on phonics.

Prefixes, Suffixes, and Roots

From grade 3 to grade 6, you can teach your child the value of prefixes, suffixes, and roots in the spelling of words. There are, however, some rules that can guide him in spelling. The following paragraphs contain some of those rules.

Verbs That End in *ize* or *ise*. Thousands of words end in *ize.* They are very common words, such as Christian**ize**, antagon**ize**, mechan**ize**, American**ize**, victim**ize**, recogn**ize**, util**ize**, and individual**ize**.

As your child studies these verbs, you can make some rules for him. For instance, after the letters *m* and *n*, he may use only *ize*, never *ise* (see the above examples).

Only a few words end in *ise*, so it's important to spend more time on them. Some of the most simple, but most confusing, words are adv**ise**, superv**ise**, advert**ise**, desp**ise**, dev**ise**, surpr**ise**, chast**ise**, and exerc**ise**.

You or your child can make a list of verbs that end in either *ize* or *ise.* If you're in doubt about the correct spelling of a word, consult the dictionary. If your child has a computer, let him run the disk containing his letter or report with *Word Plus* or *Perfect Speller.*

To Double or Not to Double. Often, your child may be confused about words that should (or should not) have a double *s*, *r*, *p*, *l*, or *n*. These words can give him double trouble. Again, here are some rules:

1. *Double s (ss).* Examples: mi**ss**pell, mi**ss**pend, di**ss**imilar, and di**ss**atisfy. As you can see, all the examples contain a double *s*, because when you attach *mis* to the word *spell*, it will contain a double *s*. However, other words that start with *mis* have no double *s* because the words to which *mis* is attached do not start with an *s*. Examples: **mis**guide, **mis**judge, **mis**interpret, **mis**inform.

When we connect *dis* to the beginning of a word that starts with the letter *s*, the new word contains a double *s (ss)*. Examples: di**ss**atisfy and di**ss**imilar.

2. *Double n (nn).* When the suffix *ness* is attached to an adjective that ends with an *n*, the newly formed noun contains a double *n (nn)*. Examples: drunke**nn**ess, thi**nn**ess.

3. *Double l (ll).* When you connect *ly* to an adjective that already ends in an *l*, the word has a double *l (ll)*. Examples: beautiful**ly**, masterful**ly**, and skillful**ly**.

4. *Double p (pp) or double r (rr).* In the case of some words with double *p*, *r*, or *s*, it's best to memorize. Examples: emba**rr**assment, hara**ss**ment, and Mi**ss**i**ss**ippi.

5. *Double r (rr), double t (tt), and other double consonants before ed.* Sometimes, it's hard to tell whether or not to double the consonant. The following are rules to remember in doubling a letter before *ed*:

a. The word must end in a single consonant. Examples: refe**r**—refe**rr**ed, compe**l**—compe**ll**ed. In the case of the word desi**st**, the *t* is not doubled because the word ends in two consonants (**st**).

b. The word must be accented on the last syllable. Examples: commit—committed, committing.

c. The word must start with a vowel. Double the consonant when adding a suffix that starts with a vowel, as long as the accent on the last syllable of the original word remains on that syllable. Example: occu**r**—occu**rr**ence. However, prefe**r** becomes preference because the accent goes back to the first syllable; thus the *r* is not doubled.

One-Syllable Words Ending in One Consonant. What should you do with one-syllable words that end in one consonant? Should you double the consonant at the end of the word when you add a suffix? Yes. The reason is simple: The rules state that when a word ends in a single consonant preceded by a single vowel (not two or more) and when the accent is on the final syllable, the consonant must be doubled. Thus, the consonant is always doubled in a one-syllable word because there's no choice. The first, last, and only syllable receives the accent. Examples: drag—dragged, drug—drugged, drop—dropped, beg—begged, run—runner.

The Addition of Suffixes. Is your child sometimes confused when he adds suffixes (such as *ly*, *ness*, and *ment*) to words that end in an *e*?

When these suffixes are added to a word, the *e* is retained. Examples: sincere—sincerely, severe—severely, immediate—immediately, measure—measurement.

When *ment* is added to words that end in *dge*, the final *e* is dropped. Example: judge—judgment.

The Dropping of e. What does your child do when he adds *able* to words that end in an *e*? Does he drop the *e* or not? Here are some rules:

1. The final *e* should be retained when words end in *ice* or *ge*. The purpose of the *e* is to keep the *c* and the *g* "soft" before the *a* in *able*. Examples: notice—noticeable,   manage—manageable.

2. The final *e* is usually dropped when words ending in *e* are preceded by any other consonant. Example: machine—machinable.

3. If a word ends in an *e* preceded by a consonant, the final *e* is dropped before any suffix that starts with a vowel. Examples: drive—driving, like—liking, arrive—arriving, live—living.

4. The *y* is considered a vowel when it is used as a suffix. Therefore, the final *e*, when preceded by a consonant, is dropped before the suffix -*y* is added. Example: stone—stony.

The Suffixes *sion* and *tion*. When the suffixes *sion* and *tion* are added to certain words, the base word may drop the final *e, t,* or *d*. Examples: educate—education, correct—correction, contend—contention.

The Vowel y. When a suffix is added to a word that ends in *y* after a consonant, the *y* becomes a vowel; then the *y* changes to an *i* and the suffix is added, beginning with a consonant. Examples: pit**y**—pitiful, happ**y**—happily, dirt**y**—dirtiness; craz**y**—crazily.

However, a few monosyllabic adjectives that end in *y* after a consonant may retain the *y* before the suffixes *ly* and *ness* are added. Examples: dr**y**—dryly, sh**y**—ness.

The Simple One-Syllable Words. One-syllable words (called monosyllables) ending in *f, l,* or *s* after one vowel usually end in double *f, l,* or *s.* Examples: bluff, ma**ll**, gla**ss.**

However, in some short words, the final *f, l,* or *s* is not doubled because it does not follow one vowel. Examples: roo**f,** coa**l,** chao**s.**

The *able* or *ible* Suffixes. These two suffixes are probably the most confusing in the English language. (These must be taught in the higher elementary grades.) There are some things to remember:

1. There are more *able* than *ible* words, so when in doubt, tell your child to use *able.*

2. The suffix *able* is usually added to a complete word. Examples: admit—admitt**able,** regret—regrett**able.**

3. The suffix *ible* is generally added to a root that is not a complete word. Examples follow:

a. Drop the final *e* and add *ible* if a word ends in *nce, uce,* or *rce.* Examples: convinc**e**—convinc**ible,** produc**e**—produc**ible.**

b. It is also used when a root word ends in *nse.* Examples: sens**e**—sens**ible,** defens**e**—defens**ible.**

c. Roots that end in *miss* always take *ible.* Example: dis**miss**—dismiss**ible.**

The Vowel Pairs *ei* and *ie*

These pairs of vowels are confusing. Your child may not easily figure out whether the *e* or the *i* comes first. Of these two combinations, *ie* is the more common, as in bel**ie**f and rel**ie**f. Words with *ei* include rec**ei**pt, rec**ei**ve, dec**ei**ve, and perc**ei**ve.

Generally, the letter *c* is followed by *ei*, rather than *ie*. (There is a short rhyme which has proven helpful to many children in solving the *ei/ie* problem: "*i* before *e*, except after *c.*")

The following are helpful guides to follow in using *ei* or *ie:*

1. If the letter *c* is pronounced as an *s*, as in re**cei**ve, it is followed by *ei*, not *ie*.

2. In certain words, *ei* is used for the long *e* sound, even if the preceding letter is not *c*. Examples: s**ēi**ze, l**ēi**sure, sh**ēi**k, prot**ēi**n, caff**ēi**ne.

3. Otherwise, *ie* is often used in syllables with long *e* sounds. Examples: bel**iē**ve, rel**iē**ve, ach**iē**ve.

The *ch-tch* Rules

The /ch/ is spelled *ch* and *tch*. (This and the items below must be taught from grade 3 to grade 6.)

1. Generally, the /ch/ sound is spelled *ch* at the beginning of a word, after a consonant, and after two vowels (**ch**in, pun**ch**, pea**ch**).

2. At the end of a syllable or a word following a single short vowel, the /ch/ sound is spelled *ch* (stret**ch**, stit**ch**). There are, however, some exceptions (mu**ch**, whi**ch**).

The *ge-dge* Rules

The /j/ sound can be spelled *ge* and *dge*.

1. Generally, the /j/ sound is spelled *ge* after a consonant (la**rge**, after a long vowel (st**āge**, and after two vowels (g**ouge**).

2. The /j/ sound is spelled *dge* at the end of a syllable or word after a single short vowel (j**ŭdge**, f**ŭdge**, and l**ēdge**).

The /ij/ Sound—Spelled *age*

At the end of a word the /ij/ sound is spelled *age* (vill**age—ij**, vant**age**, cott**age**).

Have Letters, Will Chop

In conversation or in informal writing, contractions are generally used. A contraction is a single word which comes from the combinations of two words; one letter or more letters are omitted and replaced with an apostrophe ('). You can teach contractions from grade 2 to grade 6.

Samples of Contractions

I'm—I am	isn't—is not
he's—he is	don't—do not
you're—you are	she'll—she will
they're—they are	here's—here is

You can think of many more examples—*is* to *'s*, *will* to *'ll*, *have* to *'ve*, *are* to *'re*, *is not* to *n't*, and so on.

No Linkage, No Negotiation!

Because some words are just hard to spell, your child can't always apply rules in spelling. The first thing to know about these words is the root and the meaning; then your child may be able to figure out the correct spelling. If he can't do this, just let him write down the word. From the looks of it, he may be able to determine the correct spelling. Sometimes it looks awkward when it is not spelled correctly. If the word is spelled correctly, sometimes it just looks terrific.

Take Pictures!

Some English experts say that the best spellers are those who "take pictures" of words. A good speller, they say, has seen a word correctly and remembers how it's supposed to look.

Food for Thought

Remembering these rules and following the suggestions, I hope that your child will become a good speller. I've taught them to my own children, and they have become good spellers. Your child can, too!

Perceptual Skills and Word Analysis 8

If you want your child to read well, develop in him perceptual skills and word analysis techniques, which involve *sight word* skills and *word attack* skills.

Sight Word Skills

Sight words are learned words that your child can recognize instantly. Samples of these words include *a, me, not, from, live, reach, kind,* and *today.* (See the complete list of 220 Dolch basic sight words on pages 51 – 52).

Sight Words Are Learned Words

Word Attack Skills

By having word attack skills, your child can decode a word or a group of words, pronouncing the unfamiliar words and knowing the meaning of a word, a phrase, or a paragraph. Involved in word attack skills are *configuration clues, picture clues, context clues, phonics analysis,* and *structural analysis.*

Configuration Clues. By the shape of a word, a student may know a word's pronunciation and meaning. For instance, the word *owl* can be immediately identified because the letter *w*, when placed on top of the letter *o*, is similar to the shape of an owl's head.

Picture Clues. A pupil may identify a word when it is accompanied by a picture, such as that of a Patriot antimissile missile zooming towards a Scud missile. This is why children, especially in preschool and kindergarten, should be exposed to picture books.

A Picture Is Worth a Thousand Words

Context Clues. Unknown words to a child can be identified according to its relation to the other words in a sentence. For instance, your child may not know the meaning of *angry.* But when the sentence is "The angry player broke his bat after he was struck out," he may immediately get the hint about the meaning of *angry* because of its relation to the words *broke his bat* and *struck out.*

Phonics Analysis. Since phonics involves letter-sound relationships, he can instantly identify words. Thus, he can decipher the letters or group of letters, blend the separate sounds together, and pronounce the word. Once he learns letter-sound relationships, he decodes its meaning. Since phonetic words are spelled as they are pronounced, phonics analysis also aids pupils in the correct spelling of many words.

Structural Analysis. A young child can recognize and know the meaning of a word by scrutinizing how it is constructed. To attack a word, he divides it into syllables, pronounces those syllables, and combines the sounds together. Structural analysis also helps in determining the correct spelling of words.

The Six Kinds of Syllables

A syllable can be a letter (I, a, o/range), a one small word (by, too, tie), and part of a longer word (im/pend, con/tract).

1. Closed Syllable. A syllable that ends with a consonant is called a *closed syllable.* Generally, the vowel in a closed syllable is pronounced short.

Examples

i (ĭ) in	e (ĕ) pen	a (ă) add
e (ĕ) pep	u (ŭ) cup	o (ŏ) mop
u (ŭ) tug	u (ŭ) fun	i (ĭ) kin

Remember that closed syllables may be found in one-, two-, and three-syllable words. Some examples follow:

One-Syllable Words	Two-Syllable Words	Three-Syllable Words
thĭng	pĕn/cil	ăt/tach/ment
hălf	tĭm/ber	drĭll/mas/ter
bĕg	ĭm/part	ĕn/list/ment
tĕn	ăt/las	ĕx/cel/lent
bĭg	ăt/tic	mĭs/treat/ment

There are, however, one-syllable words that are pronounced not short but long, which I call the "pretenders." You may notice that these words end in *ll, ld, ost, ind,* and *mb.* Some examples follow:

ll	*ld*	*st*
pōll	wīld	pōst
rōll	bōld	lōst
scrōll	mīld	mōst
tōll	cōld	tōast
pōll	mōld	boāst

ind	*mb*
mīnd	clīmb
bīnd	cōmb
kīnd	
fīnd	

2. Open Syllable. A syllable that ends with a vowel is called an *open syllable.* Usually, the vowel in an open syllable is pronounced long.

Examples: o (ō) no, e (ē) be, and y (ī) by.

1st Open Syllable	*1st and 2nd Open Syllables*	*Both Open Syllables*
nā/tion	dō/nā/tion	lā/dy (ē)
dō/nor	mī/crō/sphere	pō/lō
stū/dent	crē/mā/tion	sō/lō
pāper	prō/mō/tion	crā/zy (ē)
crā/yon	vō/cā/tion	jū/dō

3. The Vowel-Consonant-e Syllable. Usually pronounced long, the vowel-consonant-e syllable ends in an *e* that is silent. Some examples follow.

One-Syllable Words	*Two-Syllable Words*	*Three-Syllable Words*
māte	ter/mīte	com/plēte/ly
tīle	com/pūte	ab/so/lūte
pōle	as/sūme	ex/trēme/ly
fīre	as/pīre	pa/trōn/ize

Several endings may also be added to words that end in an *e*. Such endings are *ly, ment,* and *less. Some examples follow.*

ly	*ment*	*less*
tīme/**ly**	bāse/**ment**	nāme/**less**
nīce**ly**	plāce/**ment**	shāme/**less**

4. The Diphthong Syllable. Usually, the diphthong syllable has two vowels (t**oe**, thr**ough**), which when sounded together, produce only one sound. However, when the vowel combination is reversed (*io* instead of *oi*, or *eo* instead of *oe*), the division is made between the two vowels.

Sample Words

cu/**ri/o**	vid/**e/o**
nun/c**i/o**	me/t**e/o**r
tr**i/o**	ro/d**e/o**
pat/**i/o**	cam/**e/o**
scor/p**i/o**	Bor/n**e/o**

5. r-Combination Syllable (r-com). An *r*-combination syllable has at least one vowel followed by an *r*. Giving the vowel a unique sound, the *r* always comes directly after the vowel (*ar, er, ir, or, ur,* and *ear*).

Sample Words

sur/prise	big/**ger**
car/pool	pa/**per**
me/**ter**	beg/**gar**

6. The Consonant-le Syllable. Without any vowel sound, the consonant-*le* syllable is placed at the end of a word. In other words, only the consonant and the letter *l* are said; the *e* at the end is silent.

Sample Words

dle	*ble*	*tle*
mid/**dle**	pass/a/**ble**	lit/**tle**
pad/**dle**	drib/**ble**	throt/**tle**
med/**dle**	ter/ri/**ble**	bot/**tle**
cud/**dle**	tan/gi/**ble**	bat/**tle**
fid/**dle**	rub/**ble**	myr/**tle**

ple	*cle*	*gle*
peo/**ple**	cy/**cle**	gig/**gle**
mul/ti/**ple**	pop/si/**cle**	an/**gle**
par/ti/ci/**ple**	ob/sta/**cle**	min/**gle**
ma/**ple**	par/ti/**cle**	sin/**gie**
top/**ple**	cu/bi/**cle**	tan/**gle**

The first three syllables (open syllable, closed syllable, and vowel-consonant-*e* syllable) must be taught from grades 1 to 6, while the last three are taught from grades 3 to 6.

Decoding of Words

Your child may know the meaning of longer words for vocabulary and spelling by disassembling the words into different parts, such as separating compound words into two simple parts and other words into prefixes, roots, and suffixes.

Teach Him to Decode Words

1. Compound Words. These are the easiest to recognize because compound words are composed of two simple words. Examples:

sidewalk	toothpaste	meatball
fireproof	copyright	bookmark
warehouse	fisherman	teaspoon
earthworm	fireplace	gunboat

2. Longer Words. These word stems are from Anglo-Saxon (native English) words. Examples:

un/selfish/ly	(prefix, root, suffix)
un/selfish	(prefix, root)
selfish/ness	(root, suffix)

3. Other Words. These stems are from Latin words. Examples:

im/mature/ly	(prefix, root, suffix)
im/mature	(prefix, root)
mature/ness	(root, suffix)

Through the above decoding skills, your child can become proficient in word recognition and analysis, thereby improving his knowledge in vocabulary or spelling.

Perceptual Skills in Different Grades

How do you know if your child is below average, average, or above average in perceptual skills and word analysis? Below are some guidelines at the approximate grade levels.

★ ★ ★ ★ ★

Kindergarten

In kindergarten, your child must develop his auditory and visual skills. For example, he must be able to recognize and pronounce two- and three-syllable words, and recognize spoken words with the same initial and final sound.

Left-to-Right Eye Movement

Likewise, your child must develop the left-to-right eye movement in reading; must see the similarities and differences in sizes, shapes, and designs; and must visualize part-to-whole, for instance, by solving a ten-piece puzzle.

★ ★ ★ ★ ★
Grade 1

At this grade level, your child must know that the vowels *a, e, i, o, u,* and sometimes *y,* and the combinations of these letters, can make several different sounds (b**a**t, b**e**t, p**i**g, d**o**g, m**u**le). Likewise, he must know that consonant sounds such as *th,* can be placed at the beginning, middle, or end of a word (**th**at, wi**th**draw, wi**th**).

He should also be taught the so-called *digraphs.* The following are examples of words with vowel digraphs (two vowels with one sound):

ai	*ay*	*ea*
nail	pay	peach
tail	may	teach
mail	day	team
pail	bay	clean

ee	*ei*	*ie*
teeth	neither	tie
deep	receive	die
beef	deceit	pie
teen	seize	lie

oa	*oe*	*ou*
croak	foe	sought
soak	toe	bought
toad	hoe	though
coat	Joe	dough
foam	floe	rough

ow	*ue*	*ui*
bow	due	pursuit
window	pursue	suite
mow	cue	quick
tow	true	quiz
sow	clue	quit

Some samples of consonant digraphs (words with two consonant sounds sounded together to make one sound) follow:

ch	*sh*	*wh (hw)*
chin	sheep	what
chop	shallow	when
chart	slash	wheel
chain	mash	while
child	sheet	whine

th	th (voiced)	ng	nk
thin	**th**ud	ri**ng**	ba**nk**
sou**th**	wea**th**er	ba**ng**	sa**nk**
thing	ba**th**e	so**ng**	tha**nk**
thigh	**th**ere	lo**ng**	du**nk**

At this grade level, your child must be able to recognize word endings (such as *ly, ed,* and *ing*) and compound words, two simple words combined into one (such as football, blackboard, and typewriter). Some examples follow:

ly	ed	ing
low**ly**	want**ed**	sing**ing**
careful**ly**	penn**ed**	lov**ing**
chil**ly**	add**ed**	study**ing**
equal**ly**	tow**ed**	group**ing**

Of course, in grade 1, the child must recognize upper-and lower-case letters, words with double letters, and words with different lengths.

As a rule, the final *f, l,* and *s* are doubled when they follow a single vowel. (Also see *Spelling: To Double or Not to Double,* page 62.) Examples of these words follow:

ff	*ll*	*ss*
cu**ff**	ca**ll**	dre**ss**
sta**ff**	pa**ll**	gra**ss**
cli**ff**	ta**ll**	cla**ss**
blu**ff**	ba**ll**	gla**ss**

★ ★ ★ ★ ★

Grade 2

At this grade level, the pupil must know consonant blends such as *br* (**br**ing) and *spr* (**spr**ing). (See *Consonant Blends,* pages 17 – 18.) Examples of these words follow:

/br/	/pr/	/tr/
brush	**pr**etty	**tr**ain
brain	**pr**ay	**tr**ack
brass	**pr**ince	**tr**ee
brook	**pr**iest	**tr**ip

/dr/	cr = /kr/	/gr/
drug	**cr**own	**gr**ow
drain	**cr**ayon	**gr**een
drink	**cr**awl	**gr**ade
drill	**cr**ab	**gr**ound
dry	**cr**ook	**gr**ape

/fr/	/fl/	/bl/
frog	**fl**ower	**bl**end
fruit	**fl**ag	**bl**oom
from	**fl**at	**bl**ood
fresh	**fl**ow	**bl**eed
frozen	**fl**eet	**bl**ack

/pl/	cl = /kl/	/gl/
plus	**cl**oud	**gl**ue
place	**cl**ean	**gl**ad
plant	**cl**ear	**gl**ove
plenty	**cl**ock	**gl**ory
planet	**cl**am	**gl**ass

/sk/sc/	/sp/	/st/
ski	**sp**eech	**st**and
skate	**sp**ot	**st**ack
skin	**sp**oil	**st**udy
skid	**sp**onge	**st**ay
scarce	**sp**ace	**st**omach

/sm/	/sn/	/sl/
small	**sn**ail	**sl**ow
smell	**sn**ow	**sl**eep
smoke	**sn**ake	**sl**ip
smart	**sn**ore	**sl**am
smile	**sn**ack	**sl**ide

/thr/	/spl/	/spr/
thread	**spl**it	**spr**ing
three	**spl**ash	**spr**ay
throne	**spl**atter	**spr**ead
throw	**spl**ice	**spr**ite
throat	**spl**een	**spr**ung

scr = /skr/	/str/
scream	**str**ing
scram	**str**ong
script	**str**aight
scrap	**str**ength

Among other things, your child should learn the short vowel sounds, the use of *y* as a consonant or as a vowel (**y**ellow, repl**y**), the two sounds of *c* and *g*, the vowel and consonant sound rules, and the use of contractions. He must also learn to recognize root words and compound words. Examples of the two sounds of *c* and *g* follow:

Soft c says /s/ sound	*Hard c says /k/ sound*	*Soft g says /j/ sound*	*Hard g says /g/ sound*
cent	**c**oat	mer**g**e	**g**o
per**c**ent	**c**atalog	**G**eorge	**g**ang
cemetery	**c**amel	re**g**ion	**g**round
central	**c**olonel	lar**g**e	**g**orge

★ ★ ★ ★ ★ ★

Grade 3

At this stage of your child's school life, he must already know all the short and long vowel sounds and all the initial consonant sounds; the two sounds of *c* and *g* (**c**ent, **c**at, **g**o, **g**eography); the vowel and consonant rules; the silent letters in *kn* (**kn**ow), *wr* (**wr**ong), *gn* (si**gn**). (See *Silent Letters* on page 25.)

The Sounds of x

As a grade 3 pupil, he must be able to know that *x* is pronounced *cks* or *z* (*ta**x**,* **X**erox). If he doesn't know it yet, teach him how plurals are formed (by adding *s* or by changing *y* to *i* and adding *es*). In addition, he must know how to write and read Roman numerals from I to X. Some examples of words with the two sounds of *x* follow.

x — cks	*x — z*
*la**x***	**x**ylophone
*fa**x***	**X**avier
*Ma**x***	**x**erosis
*fi**x***	**x**erophyte

The following are examples of plural forms:

Adding s	Changing y to i and adding es
map—maps	copy—copies
pencil—pencils	sky—skies
book—books	lily—lilies
table—tables	ally—allies
computer—computers	tally—tallies

Having learned the syllabication rules, instruct your child how to hyphenate words and to use primary accent marks. (See *Syllabication Rules* on pages 26 – 27.)

★ ★ ★ ★ ★
Grades 4, 5, and 6

In the upper elementary grades, children should master the additional sounds of *a*, the /er/ sounds (*ar, er, ir, or, our*), prefixes, roots, and suffixes.

Things to Remember

You can review these subject areas with your child. Generally, they are taught in the grade levels mentioned. If he's not familiar with them, then give him the necessary time to learn them.

No doubt, if you're patient and determined to help your child master his lessons, he'll have the edge over his classmates and he'll have a good educational foundation.

9

Reading Comprehension

Reading comprehension is one of the most important things for a child to learn well in school and at home. That means that he must understand what he has read. He must be able to pick up the main and secondary ideas, make a summary of what he has read, and make his conclusion on the subject matter studied.

The four steps to comprehension competence are *picking the main idea, sequencing, grasping details,* and *drawing inferences.*

Picking the Main Idea

Picking the *main idea* of a reading selection is the process by which one looks for the subject matter or the answers to the question of *what?* Sometimes, the main idea can be determined by its title. For example, in an article entitled *The Ten Steps to Getting High Grades,* you'll know that the enumeration of a list of steps will form part of the main idea of such a selection. Sometimes, you know you're about to find the main idea by phrases such as *The most important event ... The reasons why Saddam Hussein invaded Kuwait and said, "Come and get me!" The major events that followed the invasions were... And so on.*

Sometimes, the main idea is contained in the first sentence of a reading selection. Here's an example:

> One of the worst miscalculations of Saddam Hussein about the U.S. military might was the belief that war could be won by the great number of troops in the war theater.

In short words, the *main idea* is the central thought of a paragraph or a selection; it's the author's message or what he wants to impart. In a poem, the main idea is the feeling or attitude of the poet. Generally, the main idea is revealed in the first sentence of a paragraph, the central part of the first paragraph, or the last paragraph, which forms the conclusion. Each paragraph, of course, has its own ideas, which may sometimes be the secondary ideas surrounding a central idea.

Sequencing

Sequencing is the process by which one understands the order of steps or events in any reading selection. In history, for instance, your child must arrange the events in order (for example, from the start to the end of the *War in the Persian Gulf* between Iraq and the United States and its allies). In cooking, a recipe must be followed in sequence or step-by-step procedures. Your child sometimes may know that sequential events or steps are coming when he encounters signal words such as *first, second, third,* or *then, afterwards, moreover, furthermore,* and, *likewise, besides, finally,* and many other words of that kind.

Step by Step

Develop your child's understanding of sequencing, such as in reading instruction manuals and determining the chronology of events in short stories.

Grasping Details

Grasping details is the process by which one selects the essential facts or data of a reading selection upon which all the actions are based. In a nutshell, these facts should have relationships with each other, which should be strung together by keywords or cues for easy storage in and recall from memory.

Drawing Inferences

Drawing inferences is the process by which a student understands a selection by reading between the lines and making speculations based on a few facts. In other words, such a selection has only a few details upon which one must base his answers. The student must also base the conclusion on his studies, observations, and past experiences. In short, drawing inferences is making conclusions from given facts. *Deductive* (from the general to the specific) and *inductive* (from the specific to the general) are the two types of inference. For instance, if the author writes about blooming flowers and a little warming of the weather, the reader may see in his imagination a spring day; if the writer tells about a fall day, the reader may imagine falling leaves and rain and a day that's a bit chilly.

It's Spring!

It's Fall!

If you develop the above skills in your child, there's no reason he won't be good at reading comprehension from kindergarten to the upper grades and beyond.

Subject Areas

Enumerated below are the different interests and abilities your child must master at different grade levels so he'll have an edge over his classmates in reading comprehension.

★ ★ ★ ★ ★

Kindergarten

In kindergarten, your child must have an interest in books, including picture books, and other printed matter. He must also enjoy being read to by someone else.

Preparatory to entering grade 1, teach your child to look at books from the front cover to the back cover and scan the book from the left-hand page to the right-hand page. Also, teach him that the reading of text is from left to right and from top to bottom.

Even in kindergarten, let him remember the stories read aloud to him, getting the main ideas and minor ideas, including the names of the characters.

Furthermore, he must also learn the events in progression, as if he were mentioning the events in 1-2-3 order.

Teach Events in Progression

★ ★ ★ ★ ★

Grade 1

At this grade level, the child must have the full understanding that words or printed symbols have meanings, that they represent objects, actions, or descriptions. He must also be taught well to pick the main ideas, learn the names of the characters, and draw conclusions from the facts he has read.

Teach him also that most stories being read are only imaginary events, which are called *fiction;* that is, these stories were created only in the imagination of their authors. On the other hand, tell him that there are stories or articles on events which are true, and that these are called *nonfiction.* Those stories or articles are based on current events. In telling stories, make the habit of asking or telling your child what the moral lesson is from every story read.

★ ★ ★ ★ ★
Grade 2

At this stage, develop in your child the ability to relate the pictures to the text and to predict the outcome of a story. Furthermore, hone his skills in summarizing the story in sequence and giving conclusions from facts given.

As he prepares to enter grade 3, coach him to read the table of contents, including chapter titles and subheadings and pages where he can find the specific information he seeks. (See *Previewing* on page 44 and *Skimming* on page 45.)

By this time, he must already have the ability to select books to read from the library or to buy at the bookstore. In addition, he must already show his appreciation of reading.

★ ★ ★ ★ ★
Grade 3

At this grade level, your child must already know how to classify things and information, alphabetize words by their first two letters, use charts and maps, and use the index.

For example, *classification* is the process by which similar ideas or things are put together. As discussed before, *alphabetizing* is putting together letters in A-B-C order.

Hone your child's skills in finding the main ideas, sequencing, grasping details, and drawing inferences or conclusions.

★ ★ ★ ★ ★

Grades 4, 5, and 6

In the upper elementary grades, let your child master the skills learned from kindergarten to grade 3, particularly the following:

1. Finding the main ideas and secondary ideas.
2. Remembering the events in proper sequence, including the actions or roles of the characters.
3. Using other reading techniques (see *Previewing* on page 44 and *Skimming* on page 45).

Onward to Your Child's Destiny!

Develop the above skills in your child and he'll be good at reading comprehension, an effective tool that will guide him in his total school career.

Unit III—Language Arts

Grammar and Word Usage
Hone Your Child's
  Writing Skills
Teaching Library
  and Research Skills

10
Grammar and Word Usage

It's a fact: To be proficient in speaking and writing, your child should study and practice grammar and word usage at whatever grade he is in. With a well-rounded knowledge of writing concepts and processes, he will be able to give facts and express his opinions with clarity, variety, and style.

I. Subject Areas

First, you should know what a student should be taught at different grade levels. In that way, you'll know what and how you should teach your child at a given time.

★ ★ ★ ★ ★

Kindergarten

In kindergarten, your child should be able to listen well in order to understand ideas and to follow verbal and written instructions.

Also, he should be able to express himself and to group objects and pictures into logical classifications.

Likewise, recognizing a complete sentence is a must for him. In this connection, he should know how to:

- Use nouns
- Use verbs
- Use adjectives
- Use declarative sentences
- Use interrogative sentences

★ ★ ★ ★ ★
Grade 1

Having known what a noun is in kindergarten, he should at this time learn how to change singular forms to plurals by adding *s* to many words and by changing the ending *y* to *i* and adding *es* to some other words.

He should know how to use irregular verbs, such as is/are, was/were, fly/flew, and drive/drove.

As you can see, we don't add *d* or *ed* to form the past tense of irregular verbs.

At this grade level, your child should also have the knowledge to write a sentence—combining a subject and a verb to express a complete thought.

★ ★ ★ ★ ★
Grade 2

Continue teaching the use of subjects and verbs, which are the most important parts of a sentence. As you know, a subject is the person or thing talked or written about; a verb, its partner, shows the subject's action or state of being.

The use of helping verbs or auxiliaries such as *has, have,* and *had* before verbs is emphasized at this grade level. The use of irregular verbs, mentioned in the grade I subject areas, is also continued in grade 2.

Your child should already have the knowledge of combining two sentences into one by using the so-called coordination conjunctions, such as *and, or, either...or,* and others.

Besides learning declarative and interrogative sentences, reinforce the school's teaching of composing imperative sentences and exclamatory sentences.

★ ★ ★ ★ ★
Grade 3

The addition of an apostrophe (') followed by an *s* to form singular noun possessives is already taught in school. At this grade level, be sure that your child has mastered it.

At this time, he should already be proficient in the following:

■ The use of the *s* or *es* form of the verb with a singular noun and with pronouns *she, he,* and *it.*

■ The use of the suffix *ed* to make the past tense of many verbs (walk/walk**ed**, listen/listen**ed**).

***Add* ed *to Make the Past Tense of* Walk**

■ The use of irregular verbs dr**ew**/dr**awn**, fl**ew**/fl**own**).

■ The use of a pronoun instead of a noun as a subject (Pete/**he**, Michele/**she**).

■ The use of adverbs that tell the status of something, which usually end in *ly* (slow**ly**, quick**ly**, beautiful**ly**).

★ ★ ★ ★ ★

Grades 4, 5, and 6

At these grade levels, the child should have already learned all kinds of sentences: *declarative, interrogative, imperative,* and *exclamatory,* as well as the use of all the punctuation marks.

He should have also become proficient in forming regular verbs (talk/talk**ed**) and irregular verbs (know/kn**ew**). By this time, too, he should have mastered the use of all nouns and pronouns as the subjects in a sentence.

★ ★ ★ ★ ★

II. Sentence Structure

The Types of Sentences

A Group of Words. A sentence is a group of words consisting of a subject and a verb and expressing a complete thought.

Examples:

- The **world is** round.

(In this example, **world** is the subject and **is** is the verb.)

- **John went** to school.

(Here, **John** is the subject and **went** is the verb.)

A Single Word. Sometimes, a single word or verb can also be a sentence if it expresses a complete thought. This is usually done by professional writers.

Example: Concentrate. (It is understood that a *you* precedes concentrate.)

Kinds of Sentences. The different kinds of sentences are *declarative, interrogative, imperative,* and *exclamatory.*

1. **Declarative Sentence.** A telling statement, a *declarative sentence* ends with a period.

Example: Gorbachev has a map on his head.

2. **Interrogative Sentence.** Asking a question, an *interrogative sentence* ends with a question mark.

Example: In what part of Israel did the Scud land?

3. **Imperative Sentence.** A statement giving a command or making a request, an *imperative sentence* ends with a period.

Example: You go to school today.

4. **Exclamatory Sentence.** Telling excitement or surprise, an *exclamatory sentence* ends with an exclamation mark.

Example: The marathoners are coming!

The Marathoners Are Coming!

Parts of a Sentence. As mentioned above, a sentence consists of a subject and a verb. The subject, usually placed before the verb, is the person or thing spoken or written about which may answer the questions *Who?* or *What?* The verb, which may consist of a word or a group of words, shows the subject's action or state of being. However, the part of the sentence that tells something about the subject, which may include an action verb or a linking verb, is commonly called a *predicate.*

Examples:

- The **wind is** cold.

(Here, **wind** is the subject that answers the question of *what?* and **is** is the verb. The word group **is cold** is called the predicate.)

- The **player** *hits* the ball.

(In this example, **player** is the subject and **hits** is the verb. The word group **hits the ball** is called the predicate.)

The Main Sentence Forms. The main sentence forms are (1) the *word,* the major sentence structure which serves as a part of speech; (2) the *phrase,* which represents a group of words; and (3) the *clause,* which also represents a group of words. We will discuss the phrase and the clause.

1. **Phrase.** Not containing a subject-verb combination, a *phrase* is a group of two or more words serving as a part of the sentence. (Phrases are discussed in chapter 11.) The main types of phrases are:

   a. Verb phrase
   b. Gerund phrase
   c. Participial phrase
   d. Prepositional phrase
   e. Infinitive phrase

Example: The athlete **is running.**

(Here, **is running** is the phrase.)

2. **Clause.** A *clause* is a group of two or more words containing a subject-verb combination, usually forming part of a compound or complex sentence. (The different kinds of clauses are discussed in chapter 11.) The main types of clauses follow:

   a. Independent Clause. An independent clause is a group of two or more words that expresses a complete thought.

Example: **Johnny rides the bicycle,** and **his sister plays the piano.**

b. Dependent Clause. A dependent clause is a group of two or more words that expresses an incomplete thought.

Example: **After she finished the job,** she left to see a movie. The bold-type group of words comprises the dependent clause.

Types of Sentences. The independent and dependent clauses combine to form various types of sentences. These types of sentences are as follows:

1. **Simple Sentence.** A *simple sentence,* which has an independent clause, makes a single statement. It has a subject—verb combination.

- Charles flies a kite.

2. **Compound Sentence.** A *compound sentence* is a sentence containing two or more independent coordinate clauses. Examples:

- He drives the station wagon, but he prefers the Mustang.

- Linda works during the day, and her husband goes to school at night.

3. **Complex Sentence.** A *complex sentence* is a sentence composed of one or more dependent clauses. Example:

- He waters his grandparents' plants **whenever he goes to their house.**

The **bold-type** group of words comprises a dependent clause.

4. **Compound-Complex Sentence.** Having two or more independent clauses serving as   modifiers, the *compound-complex sentence* has two or more subject-verb combinations. It has also one or more different clauses serving as modifiers. (The compound-complex sentence is too complex that it is not advisable for your child to learn in the elementary school.)

The Paragraph

A paragraph is a group of sentences with a single thought. It has a topic sentence that expresses the main idea.

The Parts of Speech

Grammar is the science of studying and analyzing the functions of words in a sentence. These sentence functions are generally known as the parts of speech, which are *noun, pronoun, verb, adjective, adverb, preposition, conjunction,* and *interjection.*

Here are definitions of the parts of speech:

1. **Noun.** A noun names or identifies a person, a place, a thing, an idea, a quality, etc. (man, book, bomb).

   a. Proper Noun. A proper noun is the name of a person or a thing (Schwarzkopf, Cuba, Buick). It is always capitalized, whether at the beginning or in any other part of a sentence.

   b. Common Noun. A common noun is any one of a class of persons, places, or things (soldier, desert, jet). Unless placed at the beginning of a sentence, a common noun does not begin with a capital letter.

   c. Collective Noun. A collective noun is the name of a group of persons or things (squad, division, branch).

2. **Pronoun.** A pronoun is any one of the class of signal words that assumes the place of a noun.

   Examples:

   My (mine), your (yours), his (his), her (hers), its (its), our (ours), and their (theirs).

   Myself, yourself, himself, herself, itself, ourselves, yourselves, and themselves.

   Who, whom, whose, that, and which.

3. **Verb.** A verb expresses action, occurrence, or state of being (is/was, are/were, goes/went, play/played).

4. **Adjective.** An adjective is a modifier that describes a noun or a pronoun (big, wide, beautiful).

5. **Adverb.** An adverb is a modifier that describes a verb, another adverb, an adjective, a phrase, or a clause (when, then, slowly).

6. **Preposition.** A preposition is a relation or function word that connects a noun or a pronoun to another element of the sentence (in, to, of, for).

7. **Conjunction.** A conjunction is a word or a group of words that connects words, phrases, clauses, or sentences (and, or, but, either...or, not only...but also).

8. **Interjection.** An interjection is an exclamatory word inserted into an utterance (Wow! What a beautiful dress.)

The Verbs

Kinds of Verbs. The two major kinds of verbs are the regular verbs and the irregular verbs. Regular verbs are those verbs whose past tense can be formed by adding *ed (talk/talk**ed**)*. Irregular verbs cannot add *ed* to past tense (speak/spo**ke**).

1. *Regular Verbs*

Examples of Regular Verbs

Infinitive	Present	Past	Past Participle
to launch	launches	launched	(had) launched
to advance	advances	advanced	(had) advanced

As you'll notice in regular verbs, the past tense and the past participle are the same.

2. *Irregular Verbs*

Examples of Irregular Verbs

Infinitive	Present	Past	Past Participle
to drive	drives	drove	(had) driven
to know	knows	knew	(had known)

In irregular verbs, the past tense and the past participle are not the same.

The irregular verb *to be* contains the verbs *is, am, are, was, were, be, being, and been.*

Linking Verb. A linking verb is a verb that doesn't show action. Its job is to link the subject with a noun, a pronoun, or an adjective.

Examples:
- My wife **is** a doctor.
- Karla **looked** pale after her speech before the class.

Verb Voices. A verb has two voices: *active* and *passive.* A verb in the *active voice* is a verb whose subject does something, while a verb in the *passive voice* is a verb whose subject gets the action.

Example of active voice:

- An Egyptian soldier killed two Iraqis.

Example of passive voice:

- Two Iraqis were killed by an Egyptian soldier.

As you can see, the above sentence was inverted to change the voice from active to passive. In the first example, the subject does something, while in the second example, the subject receives the action.

Transitive and Intransitive Verb. A *transitive verb* is a verb that needs a direct object to complete its meaning; on the other hand, an *intransitive verb* is a verb that does not need an object to complete its meaning.

Example of a transitive verb:

- He **blew** the **horn.**

In the example, **blew** is the transitive verb and **horn** is the direct object.

Example of an intransitive verb:

- The soldiers **are** coming.

In the example, *are*, a verb of *to be*, is intransitive; it doesn't need a direct object to complete its meaning.

Verb Parts. The three major parts of a verb are the present, the past, and the past participle. To form the past and the past participle in regular verbs, we have to add *d, ed,* or *t* to the present form. (Sometimes, however, the fourth part of a verb is called a *present participle.*).

Present	*Past*	*Past Participle*	*Present Participle*
walk	walked	(had) walked	walking
negotiate	negotiated	(had) negotiated	negotiating

Subject-Verb Agreement. The most common errors among students in English composition pertain to the subject-verb agreement. The rule dictates that if the subject is *singular,* the verb must be *singular, and if the subject is plural,* the verb must be plural, too. This is done in both regular and irregular verbs.

Examples:

- **He walks** slowly.
- The **U.S. commander meets** the Iraqi general in the Iraqi dessert.

In the above regular (**walks**) and irregular (**meets**) verbs, we add *s* to form the present tense.

However, in some irregular verbs, *es*, not merely *s*, is added to the verb to form the present tense for singular subjects.

Example: Michael punch**es** his rival on the nose.

Furthermore, it is understood that if the subject is plural, the verb must be in plural form; it doesn't need the addition of *s* or *es*.

Examples:

- The athletes **meet** in the gym every day.
- Peter and his group **attend** an evening class.

Verb Tenses. The verb tenses taught in lower and upper grades are as follows:

1. Present tense
2. Past tense
3. Future tense
4. Present perfect tense
5. Past perfect tense
6. Future perfect tense
7. Present progressive tense
8. Past progressive tense
9. Future progressive tense

These tenses will be discussed in the following paragraphs:

1. Present, Past, and Future Tenses

a. Present Tense. The present tense of a verb shows action that is happening at the present time (now or today).

Example: Some people view paintings at the museum.

b. Past Tense. The past tense of a verb shows action that happened in the past.

Example: Whitney Houston **sang** the Star Spangled Banner during the recent Super Bowl.

c. Future Tense. The future tense of a verb shows action that is going to happen (this afternoon, tomorrow, or any other day to come).

Example: Madonna **will get married** again soon.

Recapitulation. Here are more examples:

Present tense:	eat/eats	bark/barks
Past tense:	ate	barked
Future tense:	will eat	will bark

2. Present Perfect, Past Perfect, and Future Perfect Tenses

a. Present Perfect Tense. The present perfect tense of a verb shows action that has been completed by the present time, but without stating any specific time.

Example: The soldiers **have come** home from battle.

b. Past Perfect Tense. The past perfect tense of a verb shows action that had been completed during a definite period in the past before another happening.

Example: We **had flown** three hours before we knew that one of our companions was not on the plane.

c. Future Perfect Tense. The future perfect tense of a verb shows action that will have been completed anytime in the future.

Example: Catherine **will have been graduated** from college by the time she reaches 25.

Recapitulation: Here are more examples:

Present Perfect: has, have
Past Perfect: had
Future Perfect: will have, shall have,
                      will have been,
                      shall have been

3. Present Progressive, Past Progressive, and Future Progressive Tenses.

a. Present Progressive Tense. The present progressive tense shows action at the present time, using the *to be* verbs *is, am,* or *are* with the present participle.

Example: President Bush **is reading** the book *I've Gone to the Persian Gulf* by Dan Quayle.

(In this example, **is** is the verb and **reading** is the present participle; hence, **is reading** expresses the present progressive tense.)

b. Past Progressive Tense. The past progressive tense shows action in the past using the *to be* verbs *was* or *were* with the present participle.

Example: My girlfriend **was doing** her homework when I came.

c. Future Progressive Tense. The future progressive tense shows action in the future using the *to be* verbs *will be* or *shall be* with the present participle.

Example: They **will be meeting** in the classroom tomorrow.

Recapitulation: Here are more examples:

Present Progressive:	am writing
	is writing
	are writing
Past Progressive:	was writing
	were writing
Future Progressive:	will be writing
	shall be writing

The Rules of Capitalization

Here are some rules on capitalization:

1. Capitalize the first letter of the first word in each sentence.
2. Capitalize the word *I*.
3. Capitalize the first letter of all names of persons (Noriega, Khadafy, Baker).
4. Capitalize the first letter of the days of the week, the months of the year, and any special days (Monday, January, New Year's).
5. Capitalize the first letter of all other proper nouns such as cities, states, countries, rivers, and mountains (Farmington Hills, New York, Mississippi River).
6. Capitalize the first word, the last word, and all important words in any title, except the words *a, an, of, the, and, but,* and *nor,* and other prepositions with four or less letters, except when placed as the first word of a title (*For Dreams Must Die, The Making of an Honor Student.*)
7. Capitalize the titles of people (Dr., Mr., Mrs.)
8. Capitalize the names of languages and religions (English, Roman Catholic).
9. Capitalize the name of a nation's people (Iraqis, Israelis, Libyans).
10. Capitalize the names of significant events (The War in the Persian Gulf).
11. Capitalize the first letter of all words used in the greeting and the first word in the closing of a letter (Dear King Hussein, Lovingly yours).
12. Capitalize the names of companies and organizations (Patriot Missiles Company, Madonna Fan Club, Desert Storm Veterans Organization).
13. Capitalize the first word of a direct quotation ("Read my lips; there will be no taxes for wars," President Bush said.)

The Uses of Punctuation Marks

The following are some rules on punctuation:

1. Use a period at the end of every declarative (statement) and imperative (command) sentence.

Examples:

Statement: Brook Shields doesn't want to marry a prince.
Command: March to the war front, now!

2. Use a period after initials and abbreviations (M., V., S., Lt., Capt.).

3. Use a comma to separate the day and the year (February 14, 1991); to separate the city and the state (Detroit, Michigan); and to separate words or phrases in a series (ships, planes, and troops).

4. Use a comma before and after an appositive, to separate it from the rest of the sentence (Arthur, the valedictorian of the class, will take up medicine in college).

5. Use a comma between two parts of a short compound sentence if punctuation is needed for clarity (I have been courting her for the past several years, and I am happy that she has decided to marry me).

6. Use a question mark to end every sentence asking a question (Where are you?).

7. Use an exclamation mark at the end of an exclamatory word or sentence (Oh no! The Scuds are coming!).

8. Use an apostrophe to shorten a word or a phrase (you are—you're; who is—who's).

9. Use an apostrophe and an s to show ownership of a noun (city's water system). When a word ends with an s, put an apostrophe after the s to show possession (Jones' car).

10. Use quotation marks at the beginning and the end of direct quotations ("Come and get me!" Saddam Hussein barked.).

11. Use a semicolon to separate two closely related main clauses in the absence of a conjunction such as *and* (Terry will go to the movie; his friends will see the football game.).

12. Use a semicolon to separate clauses joined by words such as *however, hence,* and *therefore* (He didn't pass the entrance exam; hence, he can't go to college this fall.).

13. Use a semicolon to separate enumerated items if they are long or have too many commas.

Example: The candidate for the position must have the ability to use mechanical, electrical, and electronic test equipment; to provide technical supervision and guidance to supervisors and technicians; and to plan and coordinate alteration, maintenance, and repair activities with contractors, managers, and maintenance and operations supervisors.

14. Use a colon at the end of a formal greeting in a letter (Dear Sir: Dear Madam: Gentlemen:).

15. Use a colon to introduce a list (The recipe must include the following: 1 cup sugar, 2 cups lemonade, 2 pieces bread, and 5 slices meat.)

Ready, Go!

After you have rehashed the elements of word usage and grammar, you can now hone the skills of your child in English composition. In the next chapter, you can teach your child how to write a sentence in different ways and styles, thereby leading to his proficiency in writing skills.

Hone Your Child's Writing Skills 11

To be able to express himself well, you should develop writing skills in your child as early as possible. First, you need to show him how to hold the pencil or the crayon (if he's in kindergarten) and teach him to move it in the right direction to write letters in manuscript form. Then you teach him to write in cursive form. As you do this, you teach him to write a sentence, a paragraph, or a story. And remember that learning to write requires motivation, patience, and practice.

Manuscript writing should be taught in Grades 1 and 2, and cursive in the latter part of Grade 2 and in Grades 3 and 4. (See how to write the letters of the alphabet on pages 30 – 33.)

★ ★ ★ ★ ★

I. Subject Areas

The following paragraphs will explain what your child should be doing at different grade levels.

★ ★ ★ ★ ★

Kindergarten

At this grade level, your child should show interest in books and other printed matter and want to learn to write.

Left-to-Right Eye Movement

To develop his handwriting ability, demonstrate to him the left-to-right eye and hand movement. Coach him to form upper- and lower-case alphabet letters and let him copy words and sentences from what you write or from any book. Teach him to ask and answer questions and how to follow directions. Let him complete sentences orally.

Drawing Is Writing

Show him how to draw a picture. Then let him write some words describing the picture. In that way, he'll develop the skills to tell stories and experiences.

Drawing Is Writing

★ ★ ★ ★ ★

Grade 1

At this grade level, he should know that the first word in a sentence is capitalized; that initials, the first letters of names of days of the week and months, and names of persons and war equipment, such as the Tomahawk missile, are capitalized. Also let him learn that the word *I* is always capitalized, whether it's at the beginning, middle, or end of a sentence.

Punctuation Marks

Let him realize that a period is used after a sentence or a statement and after each initial. The use of a comma and a question mark, too, are taught at this grade level. To develop his composition skills, let him master writing a paragraph with a single idea.

★ ★ ★ ★ ★

Grade 2

Capital Letters

At this grade level, your child should have already mastered using capital letters in initials, names of weeks and months, titles of stories and poems, and names of streets, towns, cities, states, and countries. Emphasize that an apostrophe is used in contractions (I'll, can't, don't) and a comma is used between the day of the month and the year (February 5, 1991).

Indentation

You must see to it that he already knows how to indent every paragraph and how to write a story in sequence, from beginning to end.

★ ★ ★ ★ ★
Grade 3

At this grade level, your child should already have mastered the use of the following:

- Periods, commas, and question marks in written conversation.
- Commas after the closing of a letter and between the town or city and the state.
- Quotation marks when quoting someone.
- Apostrophes in possessive forms of nouns.

By this time, he should have already learned in school the way to expand sentences and write descriptive paragraphs. If he hasn't, then let him practice some writing at home.

★ ★ ★ ★ ★
Grades 4, 5, and 6

In the upper grades, your child should master capitalization, punctuation marks, and types of sentences: declarative, interrogative, imperative, and exclamatory.

By this time, he should already know how to compose simple, compound, and complex sentences, placing them in order in paragraphs.

★ ★ ★ ★ ★
II. How to Write a Sentence

Before your child can develop his skills in writing, he should first learn how to construct a sentence in certain ways and styles. For instance, to begin a sentence, he can use an infinitive phrase, a participle, a participial phrase, or a prepositional phrase. In other words, a sentence doesn't always begin with a subject. For this reason, learning phrases and clauses is an important process in the life of a student.

As discussed in the previous chapter, the most important parts of a sentence are the *subject* and the *verb*. The subject tells who or what the sentence is all about, and the verb tells the action that takes place.

Example: **Michelle went** to the store.

In this example, **Michelle** is the subject and **went** is the verb.

In chapter 10, we discussed the *phrase* (a group of two or more words without a subject-verb combination that forms a part of a sentence) and the *clause* (a group of two or more words containing a subject-verb combination that usually forms a part of a compound or complex sentence).

The different kinds of phrases and their definitions are as follows:

1. The Verb Phrase. A *verb phrase* is a group of two or more words containing a helping verb and a main verb.

Example: Catherine **is willing** to go to the movie theater.

In this example, **is** is the auxiliary or helping verb and **willing** is the main verb. Therefore, **is willing** is the verb phrase.

More Examples

Helping Verb	Main Verb	Verb Phrase
must	write	must write
has been	writing	has been writing
will be	writing	will be writing

Here's a list of the most commonly used helping verbs:

is	being	can
am	has	could
are	have	may
was	had	might
were	do	will
be	did	shall
been	done	should
	must	would

Generally, in a declarative sentence, the verb phrase is grouped together.

Example: Baghdad **should have been invaded** by the allied troops to force Saddam Hussein to surrender.

In this example, **should have been invaded** is the verb phrase.

However, in an interrogative sentence, the verb phrase is usually separated.

Example: **Have** you ever **been disappointed** in love?

2. The Gerund Phrase. A *gerund phrase* is a group of words containing a gerund and any related modifiers and other elements of the sentence. A *gerund* is a verbal noun that tells an action and ends in *ing.*

(Note: A. *gerund phrase* is one of the three so-called *verbal phrases:* the others are the *participial phrase* and the *infinitive phrase.* A *verbal* is a word derived from a verb that usually serves in a sentence as a noun, an adjective, or an adverb.)

Examples of a gerund phrase used as a noun:

● **Thinking** is a good habit.

In this example, **thinking** is the gerund.

● **His helping** others makes him a kind man.

In this example, **helping** is the gerund and **his helping** is the gerund phrase.

3. The Participial Phrase. One of the verbal phrases, a *participial phrase* is a group of words containing a participle and any other modifiers and other elements of the sentence. (Note: A *participle* is a major part of a verb, which may be called the *present participle* or the *past participle.*)

Regular Tense	Present Participle	Past Tense	Past Participle
talk	talking	talked	(had) talked
walk	walking	walked	(had) walked
look	looking	looked	(had) looked

a. The Introductory Participial Phrase. When the phrase is at the beginning of a sentence, it's called an *introductory participial phrase.* It may be composed of one or more words, with a comma after the phrase.

Examples:

● **Smiling**, Catherine walked onto the stage and made a speech.

● **Looking happy**, Denise accepted her achievement award from the school principal.

b. The Participial Phrase Used as an Adjective. When used as an adjective, a participial phrase can be placed following the noun or the pronoun it modifies.

Example: Two dogs, **walking on the grass**, barked at the carrier.

In this example, **walking on the grass**, placed after the subject, is the participial phrase used as an adjective.

c. *The Past Participle.* Another type of a participial phrase is the one that has a past participle. To make a past participle, we add *ed* to a regular verb with the aid of the so-called helping verbs such as *have, has,* and *had.*

Examples:

Infinitive	Past	Past Participle
to melt	melted	had melted
to finish	finished	had finished

- The ice on the pavement **had melted** when Peter arrived.
- He **had finished** reading when his friend telephoned him.

However, in using irregular verbs as learned in the previous chapter, we can't add *ed* to make the past participle.

Examples:

Infinitive	Past	Past Participle
to fly	flew	had flown
to grow	grew	had grown

- The bird **had flown** when the rains fell.
- The grass **had grown** so tall that he decided to cut it.

(1) *Describing a Noun.* A past participle is also used to describe a noun. When used as an adjective, the verb form is called a *verbal.*

Example: A **damaged** book was returned to the library.

(2) *At the Beginning of a Sentence.* A past participle may also be used at the beginning of a sentence.

Example: **Saddened** by the death of his father, the son stopped studying.

(3) *Somewhere, Somehow.* We can also place somewhere or somehow in a sentence or any participial phrase with a past participle.

Example: The bomb, **dropped** on the enemy position, did not explode.

4. The Infinitive Phrase. The *infinitive phrase* is a group of words containing an infinitive and any related modifiers and other elements of the sentence. (Note: An infinitive is a verb form usually containing the word *to* and a verb.

Examples:

- to meet: He canceled his trip abroad **to meet his girlfriend** in the city.

In this example, **to meet his girlfriend** is the infinitive phrase.

- to finish: **To finish his writing**, she did an extensive research work.

In this example, **To finish his writing** is an infinitive phrase placed before the subject *she*.

5. The Prepositional Phrase. A *prepositional phrase* is a group of words beginning with a preposition and ending with a noun or a proper noun.

Examples:

- He went **to the farm**.
- **Below the table** are some books.

The prepositional phrases are **to the farm** and **Below the table**.

(Note: The noun or the pronoun is the object of the preposition.)

Kinds of Clauses

As discussed in chapter 10, the major types of clauses are the *independent* and *dependent clauses*. (An independent clause is a group of two or more words that expresses a complete thought, while a dependent clause is a group of two or more words that expresses an incomplete thought.)

1. The Noun Clause. A *noun clause* is a dependent clause that serves as a noun in a sentence. It usually begins with words such as:

who, which, what
that, those
when, where
whatever, whichever, whoever

Examples:

- I know **that you are sad**.
- **What you have explained** is enough.

2. The Adjective Clause. An *adjective clause* is a dependent clause which serves as an adjective in a sentence. It usually begins with words such as:

which, that
when, where
who, whom, whose

Example: The woman **who looks like** Elizabeth Taylor is a Kuwaiti.

3. The Adverb Clause. An *adverb clause* is a dependent clause which serves as an adverb in a sentence. It usually begins with words that answer the questions:

When? Where?
How? Why? How much?

When? Where?

It may also have beginning words such as the following:

then, when
while, where
after, since, so that
because, inasmuch as

Example: **Since you are already here,** you may as well study your lessons.

The Use of Connectors

The Use of *And.* Sometimes there are two or more subjects in a sentence; this condition is indicated by the word *and.*

Examples:
- Michelle **and** Peter went to the store.
- Michelle, Peter, **and** John went to the store.

In the second example, **Michelle, Peter,** and **John** are the subjects and **went** is the verb. Usually, multiple subjects in one sentence are called a *compound subject.*

At the same time, we use *and* to combine two or more subjects of two or more sentences.

Examples:

- Fred wrote a story. Janet wrote a story, too.
  Fred **and** Janet each wrote a story.
- There are pencils on the table. There are books on the table. There are also some crayons and paper on the table.
  There are pencils, books, crayons, **and** paper on the table.

You'll note that a comma is placed between each item in the above example.

Also, we use *and* to combine two or more verbs or actions taken in a sentence.

Examples:

- Secretary Cheney and Brigadier General Powell flew to Saudi Arabia. Later they visited the troops in the desert.
  Secretary Cheney and Brigadier General Powell **flew** to Saudi Arabia **and** later **visited** the troops in the desert.

Secretary Cheney and **Brigadier General Powell** are the two subjects and **flew** and **visited** are the two verbs or actions in the sentence.

The subject can be the name of a person (or a pronoun—he or she or whatever), a place (Iraq), a thing (airplane), or an event (war).

In a nutshell, two or more subjects, verbs or actions, or thoughts can be combined by *and.*

The Use of *Both* **and** *Not Only...But Also.* We use *both* in front of two subjects combined, *not only* in front of a sentence, and *but also* at the middle of a sentence.

Examples:

- **Both** Bill and Charley got A's in math.
- **Not only** did the bomb destroy the bridge, **but** it **also** damaged the building.

The Use of *Or* and *Either...Or*. The words *or* and *either...or* are used to combine two or more subjects or verbs or actions.

Examples:

- Use a typewriter **or** a computer in writing your report.
- **Either** a smart bomb **or** a missile will be dropped by the plane on the enemy position.

When using the words *or* and *either...or*, make the verb agree with the subject closer to the verb.

Examples:

- An air or ground **war** *is* inevitable.
- Either the father or the **mother** *is* going to the show.
- Either the father or the **boys** *are* going to the show·
- The **house** *is* painted either brown or white.

As you can see in the third example, the word *boys* takes a plural verb (are) because it is the subject that is closer to the verb.

The Use of *Neither...Nor*. These two words are used like *either...or*. However, they express negative thoughts.

Example: **Neither** the boy **nor** the girl is eligible to participate in the contest.

Like the use of *either...or*, make the verb agree with the subject closer to the verb.

Example: Neither Johnny nor the **girls** *are* tall.

As you can see, the word **girls** is closer to the verb *are*.

Combining Two Sentences into One. Two sentences can be combined to express two related complete thoughts by using the conjunctions *and*, *but*, and *or*.

Examples:

- Secretary of State Baker flew to the Middle East. He met with Arab, Palestinian, and Israeli leaders to solve some regional conflicts.
  Secretary of State Baker flew to the Middle East **and** met with Arab, Palestinian, and Israeli leaders to solve some regional conflicts.

- The negotiations are set for next week. One member of the work group will not attend.
  The negotiations are set for next week, **but** one member of the work group will not attend.
- Give me death. Or give me money.
  Give me death or give me money.

The Use of the Semicolon

A semicolon is a punctuation mark that has a period with a comma below it (;). It is used instead of *and* to join two related complete thoughts or actions. In other words, each thought can stand alone as a sentence.

Example: He is too worried now; he is having nightmares.

Sometimes, we use *thus, therefore, however,* and other similar words after a semicolon.

Example: He has accomplished all his goals in life; however, he doesn't want to retire from his job yet.

A semicolon is used to precede words such as *for instance, for example,* and *namely,* when they enumerate certain things or actions.

Example:

- Before moving to a new city, you should consider a number of things; namely, its nearness to a school or a church, its transportation system, and its absence of smog.

The Use of the Colon

A colon is used to introduce a list.

Example: The steps are as follows: first, second, third, and so forth.

The Use of the Appositive

An appositive is a group of words that identifies or describes a person, a place, a thing, or an event in a sentence. The appositive always follows the word it identifies and is separated by commas from the rest of the sentence.

Examples:

- Margaret, **a journalist,** wrote the book.
- Baghdad, **Iraq's capital,** was heavily bombarded by allied forces' planes.
- The Stealth bomber, **the radar-proof plane,** played a major role in the war.

The Word *Having.* The word *having* can be added to the past participle of a verb, usually used at the beginning of a sentence.

Example: **Having** reviewed the book in the library, Anne went home happy.

As you can see in this example, a comma is placed after the participial phrase to separate it from the rest of the sentence.

Having can also be placed after a subject.

Example: John, **having** talked to his wife after a quarrel, went back to work.

III. Rearranging Sentences

In general, the standard English syntax in the structure of a sentence consists of the following:

subject—verb

subject—verb—modifier

subject—verb—completer (direct object or subject complement)

In other words, in writing a sentence, we usually use the above standard arrangement; for instance, the subject first, then the verb. Example:

- **Arthur talked** slowly.

Arthur is the subject and **talked** is the verb.

● Arthur talked slowly. He cited all the reasons why he didn't go to the party.

● **Talking slowly,** Arthur cited all the reasons why he didn't go to the party.

As you can see, we used the participial phrase, **Talking slowly,** placed before the subject, **Arthur,** and the other elements of the sentence.

In other words, your child, particularly at the upper grade levels, can begin sentences with participial, prepositional, or infinitive phrase and other kinds of phrases.

The purpose, of course, of pattern change is to write a story or an essay in a continuous flow of thought for clarity and style. To explain this sentence structure, let's write a biography of a fictitious person and place.

The Story of Saddam Noriega

Saddam Noriega was born in Little Desert, a small town near the city of Bunker, Virgin Islands. His parents were Isidoro Noriega, a farmer, and Milagros de la Riva, a seamstress. They were poor. They lived in a small house made of wood and roofed with dried palm tree leaves.

Saddam sold potatoes from door to door in the nearby city to help his parents cope with the hardships of everyday life. He did this every day, so he was not able to go to school during his entire life. Saddam was taught by his father to read and write in his native tongue. He wanted to be somebody in the future, maybe a leader of his town because he had big dreams.

Etc.

Of course, your child can use the above style of writing in the lower grades because he may have the tendency to always write in this manner: subject first, verb second. But as he grows older, you may teach him to use different sentence structures. For instance, he may revise the above biography as follows:

The Story of Saddam Noriega

Born in Little Desert, a small town near the city of Bunker, Virgin Islands, Saddam Noriega was the son of Isidoro Noriega, a farmer, and Milagros de la Riva, a seamstress. Being poor, they lived in a small house made of wood and roofed with dried palm tree leaves.

To help his parents cope with the hardships of everyday life, Saddam sold potatoes from door to door in the city nearby. Doing this every day, he was not able to go to school during his entire life.

However, Saddam was taught by his father to read and write in his native tongue. For he had big dreams: He wanted to be somebody in the future—maybe a leader of his little town.

As you can see in the revised version, the narration has improved a lot through the interchanging and adding of some words or phrases.

IV. Connecting Sentences and Paragraphs

As a writer, your child should know how to write paragraphs and how to connect them like chains so that his essay or story will have a compact flow of thought.

(As discussed before, a paragraph should contain a single idea or event to be supported by other ideas or events in succeeding paragraphs.)

In an essay, of course, one has to first introduce the subject or thesis to be discussed. In a short story, he may include in the introductory paragraph the problem that he wants to solve in the latter part of his written story.

Then he follows the introductory paragraph with other paragraphs to support his point of view or to narrate the events and actions of characters of his story.

However, paragraphs should have connections. Paragraph two should be connected to paragraph one; three to two, four to three, and so on—linking them together into a single, cohesive unit to form an essay or a story. This can be done through the use of so-called transitional devices.

These transitions fall into three categories:

1. Standard devices
2. Paragraph hooks
3. Combinations of standard devices and paragraph hooks

Standard Devices

The following are some examples of standard devices:

At the same time	However	But
Moreover	In fact	In addition
Consequently	On the other hand	Likewise
Of course	In other words	Even so
In general	By and large	Indeed
Admittedly	Needless to say	In fact

Many of these words can be placed at the beginning, middle and end of sentences and paragraphs.

Examples (in sentences within a paragraph):

- He didn't say anything. **However**, I could see in his eyes....

- He is poor. **In fact,** he eats only two times a day.

At the beginning of paragraphs, a writer uses transitional words or phrases, such as *at the same time, on the other hand, in general,* and so forth. Again, some words such as *however* and *of course,* may also be located, not only at the beginning of a sentence, but also at middle or end of sentences.

Paragraph Hooks

Paragraphs can be hooked together by repeating in a paragraph some words used in the last sentence of the preceding paragraph.

Example (used at the end of a paragraph):

- This can be done with transitional devices.

Example (at the beginning of the next paragraph):

Such transitional devices....

Train Cars Are Hooked to Each Other

Combinations of Standard
Devices and Paragraph Hooks

Of course, in an essay or a story, anyone can use transitional words, phrases, or paragraph hooks to connect all the paragraphs.

★ ★ ★ ★ ★

V. The Thinking and Writing Processes

After you teach your child how to construct sentences and paragraphs, he should be shown how to think about what and how he should write a particular topic.

The Processes

The processes used in writing any subject are *sequencing, observing, comparing, classifying, imagining,* and *evaluating.*

Sequencing. *Sequencing* is the process by which a writer puts ideas and thoughts on paper; for instance, in time and chronological order. In short, the flow of thoughts in an essay or order is in proper sequence, sentence by sentence and paragraph by paragraph. Of course, in a story, a writer sometimes starts with a flashback and then follows the story from beginning to end.

1. *Criteria Sequencing.* Criteria sequencing involves the organization of figures or facts through size, color, height, date, clothing, jobs, etc.

2. *Ranking Sequencing.* Ranking sequencing involves the selection of items or factors according to ranking; for instance, from the biggest to the smallest.

3. *Letter and Word Sequencing.* Letter and word sequencing involves the putting of letters or words in a specific sequence; for example, the proper placement of single words, phrases, and clauses within a sentence.

4. *Event Sequencing.* Event sequencing involves the description of different steps or actions in an essay on events or instructions.

5. *Logical Sequencing.* Logical sequencing involves the teaching of cause-and-effect relationships. Of course, with this process, the effect follows the cause; in other words, in every

effect, there's a cause. This process fits well in essays on science and history.

6. *Sentence and Paragraph Sequencing.* Sentence and paragraph sequencing involves putting sentences and paragraphs into proper order; that is, which should be first, second, third, fourth, etc.

Observing. *Observing* involves the way a writer observes people, animals, places, things, and events for the purpose of describing them on paper. If your child wants to describe a certain animal, he has to see how it opens or closes its eyes, how it scratches its own body, how it walks, and how it eats.

Comparing. *Comparing* involves the process by which a writer makes comparison through the use of the so-called figures of speech—similes and metaphors. For example, your child may say, "Your lips are like red roses blooming in the midst of spring," or "He is as crazy as Saddam Hussein."

How to Compare

Classifying. *Classifying* involves sorting items or putting things into certain categories; for instance, similar things (in size, shape, or color) in each category.

Imagining. *Imagining* requires the writer to create in his reader's mind an image of what he's talking about; for instance, the story's setting, plot, and characterization.

Imagining Creates Visions

Evaluating. *Evaluating* requires the writer to know how to present facts, opinions, logic, and emotions in order to persuade others to do something or to have belief in his thesis.

1. *Facts and Opinions.* Through this process, the writer should know the difference between facts and opinions.

2. *Persuasive Writing.* For instance, a student may write letters to President Bush as to why he may not use nuclear weapons to defeat his enemies. Of course, to do so, he should express his valid reasons to prove his point against the use of nuclear weapons.

3. *Emotional Writing Versus Objective Writing.* With this process, the writer evaluates his writing, whether he has appealed to emotions or focused his attention on facts without any emotional appeal.

The Written Work

Prewriting. *Prewriting* is the time when your student thinks about what he should write. While thinking about it, he may or may not discuss the matter with you or anybody else. In other words, prewriting is the time when he outlines in his mind and on paper what he should be writing.

Drafting. Drafting is when writing actually starts. Your child then puts down on paper what is in his mind: just let him write, write, and write. The main point is, he should try to put all the important data and facts he wants to be included in a descriptive paragraph or story. The commas, periods, and other punctuation marks are just put in, to be corrected later if there are any mistakes. Grammar, too, should be taken seriously later. When this copy is finished, it's called a rough draft.

Editing. After he has read his story or short essay, he may reread it or show it to his classmates (and teacher). Then he changes some words or rearranges some sentences to make the story clearer. That's editing.

Writing Procedures

Here are the procedures followed in writing workshops in elementary schools as part of a whole-language program.

1. The teacher and each student read alone.

2. The student makes notes of what he or she has read in a log or a journal, while the teacher makes notes on how the students are doing in reading and note-taking.

3. Then the teacher and the students hold a meeting, a *reading conference*, where they discuss what they have read.

4. The teacher and the students, in a *book-experience period*, share their feelings and opinions on their respective topics.

5. The teacher then conducts a writing workshop in which students are taught how to think like writers, writing on subjects they select from their experience.

6. Then students edit their own works among themselves or with the help of their teacher.

7. Then they bind their books and post their written works on the bulletin board. They call that *publishing.*

Conclusion

In teaching your child to write sentences, point out to him that if he's not satisfied with what he has written, he can invert some sentences and place the phrases and clauses at the beginning, middle, or end of the sentence. To make the article or story flow smoothly, he has to use connectors such as *and, or,* and *either...or* at the beginning, middle, or end of sentences. He can also use words such as *moreover, on the other hand, in general,* etc., to put paragraphs in proper sequence.

Writing is an art to be learned but it can be attained by practice: *writing* and *editing.* Practice makes perfect! Who knows? Your child may become a future Stephen King or Danielle Steele!

The Writer at Work!

Teaching Library and Research Skills 12

To be an "A" student, your child should acquire library and research skills to skillfully do his assignment or to write a report or a research paper. Teach him the good habit of going often to the library, especially during the weekend. If he forms that habit, using the library will be fun, enjoyable, and rewarding. Thus, reading will be an important part of his everyday life—from childhood through adulthood.

Of course, the first thing to do is to get a library card for your child. Usually, if he is below sixteen, the card needs your signature as a parent or a guardian.

★ ★ ★ ★ ★

I. Subject Areas

The abilities and knowledge your child should acquire to learn library and research skills at different grade levels are discussed in the following paragraphs.

★ ★ ★ ★ ★

Kindergarten

Preparatory to Grade 1, your child must know that books, pamphlets, magazines, and other materials are found in specific orders and places in the library.

At this time of his life, he must already know the following:

■ That the library is for young and old.
■ That picture books and storybooks abound in the library.
■ That there are several book sections in the library, including one for children.

★ ★ ★ ★ ★
Grade 1

At this grade level, the student should already have an initial understanding of the difference between fiction and nonfiction books.

He must also know that besides books and magazines, other reading and audiovisual materials abound in the library.

Among other things, he should be able to:

■ Decide which books to read.

■ Identify the book's front and back covers, including the spine and its label.

■ Read the title page and copyright page.

■ Attend any storytelling program or audiovisual presentation.

★ ★ ★ ★ ★
Grade 2

At this grade level, he should already know how and where to find any book by the author's last name.

Among other things, he should also be able to:

■ Know the difference between fiction and nonfiction books.

■ Read picture books, dictionaries, and encyclopedias.

■ Summarize short pictorial stories.

■ Participate in group discussions on storytelling programs or audiovisual presentations.

★ ★ ★ ★ ★
Grade 3

Your child in Grade 3 should already know that all materials in the library are located through the use of call numbers on cards.

He must be familiar with the reference section, where he can find books such as dictionaries, encyclopedias, atlases, and almanacs. He must also learn to locate a specific word or topic in any particular book, dictionary, or encyclopedia.

He should also have the knowledge to find city, state, and national periodicals.

Among other things, your child should be able to:

■ Read table of contents, the preface, the foreword and other parts of the book.

■ Know the difference between the various types of literature.

★ ★ ★ ★ ★

Grades 4, 5, and 6

At these grade levels, your child should be able to do research work in the library almost without any help from you or any library assistants. In other words, he should already be totally independent in his research work.

As a whole, he should be able to:

■ Take notes, outlining and summarizing what he has read.

■ Understand fully the difference between fiction and nonfiction.

■ Find and use references such as dictionaries, encyclopedias, periodicals, and audiovisuals.

★ ★ ★ ★ ★

II. Definitions

But before proceeding any further, we must define
words to pave the way to understanding library and research
skills.

1. Glossary—a brief dictionary that includes words related to
a specific topic or subject, usually located at the end of a book.

2. Abridged dictionary—a dictionary that contains words in
common use.

3. Unabridged dictionary—a dictionary that tries to compile
all words in the English language.

4. Atlas—a book that contains maps which may include
tables, charts, and illustrations. Part of an atlas is an index.

5. Encyclopedia—a book or a large set of books or volumes
that gives information on many branches of knowledge. Each
book has a number and guide letters on its spine to locate
subjects. One of the volumes is an index.

6. Map—a drawing that represents a plane surface of a region
or regions, or a country or countries, including cities, bodies of
water, mountains, etc.

7. Chart—a sheet containing a group of facts about something in the form of graphs, diagrams, and tables.

8. Table—an arrangement of related facts and figures in
order sequence, usually in rows and columns.

9. Graph—a diagram that uses numbers, curves, broken
lines, or a series of bars to show relationship between things.

10. Index—the section of a book that alphabetically lists
names, subjects, etc., together with the page number where
they appear in the text. It is located at the end of an encyclopedia
or a nonfiction book.

11. Card catalog—a catalog that consists of author cards,
subject cards, and title cards, all filed in alphabetical order. Any
title starting with A, An, or The is filed alphabetically in accord-
ance with the second word in the title.

12. The Dewey Decimal System—a standard system that is
used for library book classification. Devised by Melvin Dewey in
1876, the system assigns numbers to designate general categories composing ten main groups, each with subdivisions.
This number is a *call number,* which simplifies book selection
and organizational systems in libraries. Example: 200 – 299—

Religion, a main group (with one of its subdivisions being 297—Religions of the Far East).

13. Gazetteer—a geographical dictionary that alphabetically lists place names throughout the world, which may include rivers, lakes, mountains, reefs, bays, regions, islands, cities, and states.

14. Almanac—a book, usually published yearly, that includes statistical information on almost any subject.

15. Spine—the part of a bound book that covers the text's backbone and contains the title, the author's last name, and the publisher's name or logo. The book's call number is stamped on the spine.

16. Table of contents—the section in the front of a book that lists the chapters, and sometimes the subject areas included in them, and the pages where to find them.

17. References—books that are used as guides or references and cannot be taken out of the library, such as study aids, encyclopedias, dictionaries, and atlases.

Conclusion

There's a whole world of fascinating subjects in the library. But access to that world is limited unless a person knows how to use the library to its fullest potential.

Therefore, learning library and research skills is an important part of a student's life. If you expose your child to the myriad of reading materials in the library and teach him the value of reading, there's no doubt that he will grow up as a successful student and future career person.

Unit IV—Science

**Introduction to
the Study of Science**

How Animals Live

How Plants Live

Earth and Space

Physical Science

Introduction to the Study of Science 13

Science is an integral part of a human being's life. In fact, science provides an understanding of natural phenomena and helps us to solve the problems of everyday living. That's why it is one of the major subjects in school.

In addition, a nation's advance in modern technology depends on science and scientific benefits. For instance, inventions play a large role in a people's way of life and in dealing with other nations of the world—in war or in peace. In fact, the use of modern technology by the United States in 1991 resulted in winning a war against Iraq.

Moreover, science is useful and meaningful to students. Through the study of science, they can do creative thinking, solve problems, gather information, experiment, and draw conclusions based on existing facts and figures. Another thing, by studying science, students can understand the living and nonliving things around them and how to use them for their own benefits.

Major Science Units

In the next four chapters, we will discuss the three major units of science:
- Life Science (Plants and Animals)
- Earth Science (Earth and Space)
- Physical Science

The Senses

The senses—*seeing, hearing, smelling, tasting,* and *feeling*—are very important tools in the study of science. For this reason, you must teach them to your child.

133

1. **Seeing.** Humans use the *eyes* for seeing (of course, animals do, too). The eyes are the radars of the human body. Some people may shout, "A Scud is coming! A Scud is coming!" Then the message reaches the brain that orders the body, "Run!"

When light reaches the eyeball, nerves transmit the light to the brain, and then—you see! "I see it!" you may say. Your eyelids, of course, may close and open—like the lids of the front lights of some automobiles. The eyes see different shapes, sizes, and colors. They may watch MTV with Madonna or Mariah Carey on the television screen—singing, dancing, and yelling. They see them all!

2. **Hearing.** The *ears* are used for hearing. "Better listen," you may say to your child. "If not, you won't master this lesson!" The message is transmitted to your child's brain by his ear nerves. Then the brain orders the body to do what it needs to do. But, of course, the brain does the remembering itself by storing the information in its own warehouse.

The ears hear low and high sounds. They hear all sorts of sounds: "Boom! Boom! Bang! Bang! Zing! Zing!" They come from all directions—music, noises. You name it, you get it!

3. **Smelling.** The *nose* is used for smelling. "There's a skunk!" may be the message the nose nerves carry to the brain. Then the brain orders the body to close the nose with either of your hands.

The nose can determine if a smell is bad or good. And, of course, we like good smells—the smells of perfume or fresh air or good cooking.

4. **Tasting.** The *tongue* is not only used for making sounds or speech, but also for tasting. It tastes food before it enters the human body. That's because the tongue has little bumps called *taste buds*, which are the tongue's tasters. For instance, taste buds on the tip of the tongue can taste sweetness. Next come the buds for tasting saltiness, located at both sides of the tongue near the tip. Then come the buds for tasting sourness, which are at both sides of the tongue near its innermost part. Bitterness can be determined by the buds at the inner part near the throat before the food goes into the stomach—but sometimes, it's too late, it's going, going, going, gone! (Before, I hated to see the bumps on my tongue; now, I know the reason why the surface of the tongue is rough.)

5. **Feeling.** The *skin* of the human body may be white, black, brown, yellow, or colors in between. But whatever color it is, it can feel the hotness, the coldness, the dryness, the smoothness, the roughness, the wetness, or whatever of so many things. In fact, when two persons—a man and a woman—touch each other with their hands or lips, they know if they are in love or out of love. This is because when the skin feels something—ecstasy or danger—nerve cells for different kinds of feelings shoot the message to the brain. Then the brain tells the body to do the appropriate action or actions.

Science Processes

Science processes are categories like the following:
1. Observing/Identifying
2. Classifying
3. Measuring
4. Sequencing/Ordering
5. Inferring
6. Predicting
7. Communicating
8. Investigating
9. Controlling Variables
10. Formulating Hypotheses
11. Interpreting
12. Defining
13. Formulating

Students must have skills in the above 13 processes so that they can

■ give definitions of words commonly used in science, enabling them to know what they are doing and what they are supposed to do;

■ get explanations and clear views of common phenomena in science; and

■ apply processes and creative thinking in the study of science.

1. **Observing/Identifying.** One must either *observe* or *identify* objects or things (animals and plants, too) by using the senses. This is done through the eyes, the ears, the nose, the tongue, and the skin.

2. **Classifying.** *Classifying* is the process by which objects, living things, and nonliving things are grouped together into certain classes, according to their similarities and differences in sizes, shapes, and colors.

3. **Measuring.** *Measuring* is the process by which instruments are used to get quantitative information, such as an object's length, width, or diameter.

4. **Sequencing/Ordering.** *Sequencing* and *ordering* are the processes by which objects, things, and events are arranged in sequence or order, such as *first, second, third,* and so forth or according to size or color.

5. **Inferring.** *Inferring* means that one must explain his or her observations of certain things or events.

6. **Predicting.** *Predicting* is the process by which one must tell in advance what will or may happen based on the results of observations and inferences.

7. **Communicating.** *Communicating* is the process by which a student must communicate with his peers or teachers about observed events by means of written words, drawings, graphs, or charts.

8. **Investigating.** To *observe* and *investigate* certain events or activities, a student must do some tests and experimentations to be able to gather certain facts and figures.

9. **Controlling Variables.** *Controlling variables* is the process by which variables are identified by manipulating one variable at a time, while others are controlled, in order to determine the specific cause and effect of certain activities or events.

10. **Formulating Hypotheses.** *Formulating hypotheses* is the process by which one must explain or give reasons for the cause of any results of an observation or an experimentation based on given facts.

11. **Interpreting.** *Interpreting* is the process by which patterns among sets of data are examined, which may result in the stating of inferences, predictions, or hypotheses.

12. **Defining.** *Defining* means one must create or establish a definition by describing an experience or experiences about certain activities.

13. **Formulating.** *Formulating* is the process of developing a mental perception of an object or a phenomenon based on a synthesis of sense impressions.

One, Three, or Five
Processes at a Time

The 13 processes are not all used at the same time. One, three, or five processes are normally used at a time. The use of certain processes depends on the objectives for certain projects or activities.

For instance, there are times when a teacher wants only to use observing/identifying, inferring, investigating and interpreting processes in a certain project.

Conclusion

Now we have realized the importance of science in our daily life. In fact, our way of living depends much on what benefits science can give us. In view of this, the study of science should be done from kindergarten on to the upper grades. It should bring fun, enjoyment, and rewards to your child. But it should be done not only in school and during science field trips, but also at home—with your guidance and teaching.

Indeed, the study of science, like life itself, is an adventure!

How Animals Live 14

Humans are not the only inhabitants of Planet Earth. Other living things, animals and plants, are our neighbors, friends, and, sometimes, enemies. We share with them the Earth's resources. We give plants carbon dioxide, and they give us oxygen. We eat some animals; sometimes, some of them eat us, too. In a nutshell, whether we like it or not, they are our Earth mates—though they be friends or enemies. That's why we need to study how they live, how they produce, and how they die.

For the purpose of teaching your child about living things, the following paragraphs describe what is taught in school at different grade levels.

Subject Areas

★ ★ ★ ★ ★

Kindergarten

In kindergarten, your child should learn about the different kinds of animals and seeds of plants. For instance, he must learn how animals and plants grow—where they come from, where they live, and where they usually travel as invaders or tourists.

Animals

In the study of animals, your child must be able to identify both wild and tame animals and classify them by environment and habitat. Likewise, he should be able to classify them into groups according to size, shape, and color.

Plants

In the study of plants, he should learn to categorize seeds by properties and to identify plants in your town or city. Also, he must learn why plants are important to human beings.

The use of the senses (seeing, hearing, feeling, tasting, and smelling) is very important in the study of science—particularly in the study of living things. It is through these senses that your child observes, identifies, and measures animals or plants. For these reasons, you must teach him how to use his senses.

★ ★ ★ ★ ★

Grade 1

At this grade level, your child continues to learn about the kinds of animals and plants and the use of the senses needed to study science.

For example, he should be able to identify and classify animals according to their habitat and care for their young. In addition, he should be able to identify domestic and wild animals. In the case of wild animals, he must know how they move from place to place in their everyday living in search for food or mates.

In the study of plants, let him identify the five important parts of a plant: *root, stems, leaves, flowers,* and *fruits* (if any). Furthermore, he should be able to identify the seeds of vegetables, fruits, and other trees.

★ ★ ★ ★ ★

Grade 2

In this grade, your child should be able to describe where and how animals and plants live.

In the study of animals, he should study the animals of long ago, such as the dinosaurs.

For instance, knowing how animals reproduce is important. He should learn

■ the difference between mammals that reproduce baby animals that look like them and animals that are hatched from eggs; and

■ that some animals reproduce their own kind of offspring (that is, they look alike), while other animals produce through *metamorphosis*—the creation of living things that undergo different processes (i.e., from eggs to baby animals).

In the case of plants, he should learn the different kinds of plants. Examples are those plants that thrive well in wet and dry seasons. Learning wood layers is also a must for your child because through wood formations, he will be able to know how old a tree is.

★ ★ ★ ★ ★

Grade 3

At this grade level, your child should know the life cycles of animals and the importance of animals to man.

The identification of animal habits, natural or man-made, is a must. At the same time, teach him the steps being undertaken to protect the so-called endangered species.

In the case of plants, he should learn how seeds travel and grow in different kinds of location, soil, and weather. Also, point out to him the importance of trees in the ecological system. As many books say, "Save the Earth!"

He should also learn the importance of animals to man and why some animals are harmful to man.

★ ★ ★ ★ ★

Grade 4

At this grade level, your child should learn the classification of plants and animals. For instance, knowing how animals live together is a must. How living things survive in certain places or environments should also be taught thoroughly.

★ ★ ★ ★ ★

Grade 5

In this grade, the activities of green plants are usually taught. At the same time, your child should already be familiar with animals with backbones (the vertebrates) and without backbones (the invertebrates).

In living communities, it is also a must for him to learn how predators (the attackers that eat their fellow animals) and the preys (the animals that are hunted by fellow animals for food) coexist in their habitats.

★ ★ ★ ★ ★
Grade 6

In this grade, your child should already be familiar with plant growth: how they grow, how they reproduce, and how certain plants are adapted to certain climates or regions. Examples are the cactus and other desert plants.

In the case of animals, he should learn how animals adapt to certain habitats controlled by certain weather conditions and why certain animals, like birds, go to certain places of the Earth in winter or whatever kind of season in which they migrate.

✴ ✴ ✴ ✴ ✴

Plant and Animal Classification

To study plants and animals, scientific classification is used to divide them into related groups.

Taxonomy is the science of classifying living organisms. They are divided into the following major groups: *kingdom, phylum, class, order, family, genus,* and *species.*

Kingdom, the largest among the groups, is divided into three subkingdoms: one-celled animals, animals with digestive organs, and animals with no digestive organs.

The seven classification groups are:

1. **Kingdom.** It is the largest among the groups.

2. **Phylum.** Members of this group are said to have common ancestors (those animals that lived long ago).

3. **Class.** An animal's class is based on the kind of its outer covering or how it feeds its young.

4. **Order.** This classification among mammals depends on their major food sources, such as plants.

5. **Family.** This refers to animals that have much in common, but it doesn't mean that members of different genuses are compatible and are capable of producing their own offspring.

6. **Genus.** Members of a genus look similar; however, different species cannot make love or bear their own offspring.

7. **Species.** A species is the smallest group of animals which are able to breed among themselves, but not with members of any other species.

Of the above-mentioned classification groups, we shall discuss the third group, *class.* But before we discuss the classes of animals, we shall define the words *vertebrate, invertebrate, cold-blooded,* and *warm-blooded.*

Vertebrate and Invertebrate. Animals are also grouped into two classifications: *vertebrate* and *invertebrate.* Animals with backbones are called *vertebrates.* Those without backbones are called *invertebrates.* (The backbone is the column of bones at the back of certain animals made up of separate bones connected by the spinal cord, ligaments, and disk-shaped cartilage.)

Cold-Blooded and Warm-Blooded. *Cold-blooded* animals are those whose body temperature adjusts to the environment's temperature. *Warm-blooded* animals are those whose body temperature remains relatively the same, regardless of the environment's temperature. Insects and amphibians are examples of cold-blooded animals, and mammals and birds are examples of warm-blooded animals. (Humans are warm-blooded creatures.)

However, before we proceed, let's define what an animal is. An animal is a living thing that is an animal eater (carnivorous), or a plant eater (herbivorous), or both carnivorous and herbivorous (omnivorous), or an insect eater (insectivorous). It's either a vertebrate or an invertebrate and either cold-blooded or warm-blooded.

You don't want to be called an animal. Neither do I. But the fact is, according to science, we are animals, but animals of the highest group. We also belong to another classification: the so-called *primate group,* which includes apes, monkeys, and lemurs. But that doesn't mean that we are monkeys. It simply means that members of this group are characterized by flexible hands and feet.

Have Company, Will Travel

Some animals are loners, but most of them like to be in groups. For instance, bees, ants, wasps, and other small creatures live in colonies or swarms. Fish travel in schools or shoals. Whales live in herds or gams. Birds congregate in flocks.

The Classes of Animals

1. Milk-Fed Mammals

Mammals are warm-blooded vertebrates (with backbones) that are nursed with their mothers' milk. Human beings are classified as mammals, although many are nursed on other animals' milk.

Here are some characteristics of mammals:

■ They have skeletons which have at least 200 bones.

■ They have hair, although some become bald or hairless when they become middle-aged or old.

■ They may be carnivorous (animal eaters), herbivorous (plant eaters), omnivorous (both animal and plant eaters), or insectivorous (insect eaters).

■ They have more highly developed brains than other animals.

■ Most live on land, but a few live in the ocean, such as whales and porpoises.

A Right Whale

2. Birds

It's not a plane! It's not Superman! It's a bird!

Birds are warm-blooded, vertebrate animals with wings and fly in the air like airplanes.

The characteristics of birds are:

- They lay eggs.
- They have two legs.
- They have two wings.
- They have beaks.
- Their bodies are covered with feathers.
- They are warm-blooded.

About 8,600 species of birds live in every part of Planet Earth—underground, on land, above ground, in trees. They live everywhere. But, of course, they fly over the oceans during their way to and from migrations.

All birds have wings, but they can't all fly. For instance, penguins can't fly, although they use their wings for swimming underwater. So some birds just walk and run; others can fly a little bit over the ground, such as chickens.

A Rooster and a Hen

Why They Can Fly. Birds can fly because they are born with strong bones and muscles. Their wings and bodies are aerodynamically designed for flying. They also have efficient lungs that can support oxygen for a long time and a digestive system that can digest food and release energy quickly.

Birds take off in different ways; however, most lift-off methods involve the vigorous flapping of the wings, unlike planes that don't flap their wings while taking off from the runway. Other birds take off from a high point—then fall into the air and spread their wings.

A White-Tailed Eagle

How Birds Reserve Energy. Sometimes we wonder why birds don't get tired while flying. Birds know how to reserve energy. In fact, they don't flap their wings all the time because they have special flying techniques. For instance, when the Sun's heat warms the air at ground level, the air tends to rise, resulting in an upward thermal current. Then birds such as eagles take advantage of those currents to soar. They flap their wings only when they move from one thermal current to another. Then with outstretched wings, they glide like a skier who glides down the ski slope. When the birds are near the ground, they soar with the help of the wind and then glide again—repeating the cycle over and over.

The largest bird, the African ostrich, has a height of about 8 feet and weighs up to 300 pounds.

3. Fish

Fish are vertebrate animals that live in fresh or salt water. The parts of a fish include the *head*, the *trunk*, and the *tail*. The smallest fish, the goby fish, is less than half an inch long, while the largest fish, the whale shark, may weigh up to 15 tons!

Fish of the Cod Family

Fish swim by using their tail fins; other fins are used in maneuvering and balancing. They receive dissolved oxygen in water by playing the water over their gills.

4. Scaly Reptiles

Reptiles are cold-blooded vertebrate animals covered with dry and scaly skin. They breathe through their lungs. Some examples of reptiles are the turtle, the tuatara (similar to a lizard), the snake, and the crocodile.

Most reptiles are carnivorous (meat eaters), but some are herbivorous (plant eaters).

Ordinary lizards, which are also considered reptiles, have four legs, long tails, movable eyelids, and ear openings (but no outside ears like humans have). However, some lizards have no legs at all.

Another reptile is the snake. Even without legs, it can easily chase a human being, especially on grass. "Here I come!" it seems to say as it moves in s-formations while chasing you.

Eastern and Western Diamonback Rattlesnakes

5. Two-World Amphibians

Amphibians are animals with backbones that are capable of living both on land and in water. Some examples of amphibians are frogs, toads, and salamanders.

The characteristics of amphibians are:

- They have four legs.
- They hatch from jelly-covered eggs.
- Most of them lay eggs in water.
- They live on land as adults.
- They have moist skin.

Like human beings, frogs and toads have hearts, lungs, livers, stomachs, intestines, and bladders. While similar in looks, frogs and toads are entirelay different animals. Frogs have smooth, wet skin and live in or near water. On the other hand, toads have rough, bumpy skin and live on land; they go to water only to lay eggs. Also, they move slower than frogs.

Baby amphibians breathe through their gills, while most adult amphibians breathe with their lungs.

Tadpoles are young frogs and toads which lose their tails when they reach adulthood. The majority of frogs or toads can use suction cups on their toes in climbing trees and hanging upside down. "Look, Ma, I'm upside down!" one might be saying while doing it.

Development of a Frog From Tadpole to Adult

The salamander is the largest amphibian. In fact, it can weigh up to 100 pounds. Although some never develop lungs, the salamander is capable of breathing through its skin. And one wondrous thing about the salamander is that it can regrow any missing legs or tail.

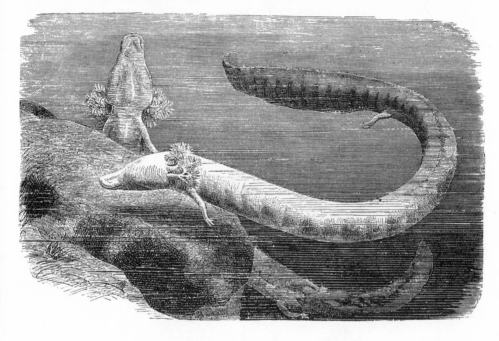

Olm, or European Blind Salamander

Amphibians, unknown to many people, shoot a poison when they are attacked. This poison can kill or scare away their enemies.

6. Swarming Insects

Insects are invertebrates with six legs. They are also called six-legged *arthropods*.

The characteristics of insects are:
- They have six legs.
- They have a jointed body.
- They have an antenna.

- They have three body parts.
- They are cold-blooded.
- They have outer skeletons.

■ An insect's skeleton, called the *exoskeleton,* is outside its body, not inside.

An insect's body is divided into three parts: the *head,* which contains mouthparts used for sucking, piercing, chewing, or lapping (drinking liquid by dipping it up with the tongue like a dog); the *midsection,* which contains the thorax to which the legs and the wings are attached; and the hind part, called the *abdomen,* which contains organs for digestion, elimination, and reproduction.

Most adult insects have two eyes with separate lenses and two antennae which are used for smelling, feeling, and sometimes tasting and hearing.

An insect's feet are used for jumping, digging, and swimming. It usually has two sets of wings; the first is connected to the middle of the thorax, while the second is behind that.

Some insects are just amazing! Imagine, a dragonfly can move as fast as a slow-moving car, about 25 miles an hour. A grasshopper can jump about 20 times the length of its body. A fly can walk upside down by using the suction pads and hooks on its feet. What wonders!

Many Types of Flies

Parading Ants. Most of the time, when you stroll on your lawn or in a park, you see some ants. They are on parade! If you follow them, you'll see an ant hill, which is like a small pile of dirt. At the middle of the hill is a hole which ants use to enter and exit from the hill. Yes, it's called an ant hill, but to Saddam Hussein, it is a bunker.

Section of an Ant Hill

However, some ants live in old timbers; some species live in trees or in hollow stems. They are usually yellow, brown, red, or black in color.

Ants live in a society. They are queens, males, or workers. The queens reproduce the offspring. When a queen lays eggs, the female workers take them to the "nursery." Weeks later, the eggs are hatched as *larvae*. Then the larvae *pupate* and spin themselves into silken cocoons, which, at maturity, become *adults*.

Ants have a certain way of communication. They communicate by feeding mutually or "kissing." They not only give food to each other, they also give some kind of secretions.

Wood Lovers. Termites, which sometimes are called white ants, are really not ants at all. While ants have a thin waist between the thorax and the abdomen, the termites have a larger body.

Like ants and bees, termites live in a society, as they like to live and work together. "We are a family!" they might say.

Three caste of termites are typical—reproductives, workers, and soldiers.

The king and the queen reproduce offspring. The female workers build their huge nests or mounds, which have intricate interiors, and gather food.

The soldiers with large heads and jaws fight other ants and other invaders with their built-in weapons. The workers are sterile soldiers. Being blind, the soldiers are not afraid of their enemies, regardless of the latter's size.

Both sexes are present in equal numbers, but only the king and the queen have fully developed sex organs. The queens, which are the largest termites, have the duty to populate the Earth with termites, resulting in the fact that they do nothing but lay eggs. It is said that some queens can live like humans— about 50 years! So imagine how many millions of termites they can produce in a lifetime!

Many termites feed on wood. But they don't actually digest the wood. Inside their bodies abound microscopic animals called *protozoans* that digest their food.

Of course, some termites build their huge mounds on the ground, particularly in tropical and subtropical places. The termites break off their wings when they move to another place. Just why they do that, the scientists don't yet know. I don't, either.

Buzzing Bees. Bees live in a group, called a *colony*, in a house of their own, called a *hive*. For instance, honeybee colonies are located in self-made nests, with one hive usually containing thousands of bees.

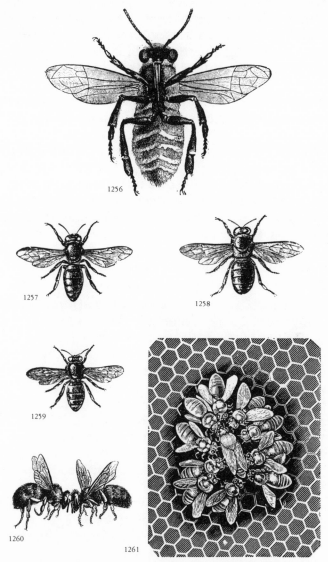

1256: A Species of Bee. 1257–1261: Honey-bees (1257–1259) Show Queen, Male and Worker, respectively).

Three kinds of bees live in a colony: the queen, the workers, and the drones. The workers are produced from fertilized eggs and are fully equipped to gather nectar, make honey, and take care of the hive. The drones are born from unfertilized eggs, and they are the ones that make love with the queen. Like other insect queens, the bee queen lays all her eggs in the colony.

It's puzzling, but the workers, which are all female bees, have no way of reproducing; they have to build the hive and make the honey. Most of the time, they also take care of the baby bees for the queen.

Of course, bees are great attackers, like those that attacked school children inside a bus as seen in a movie whose title I have already forgotten. The best way to avoid the sting of buzzing bees is to dive, but be sure that the place where you dive for safety has enough water.

Wasps. Like bees, wasps bodies have three parts. But unlike the stockily built bees, wasps have slender, hairless bodies. Some example are wood wasps, cedar-wood wasps, and parasitic wood wasps. Members of some groups are solitary; however, large numbers of some species make nests together in a small area. Some build nests on the ground or in branches of trees, the nests being made of paper-like materials.

Flying Leeches. Mosquitoes may be called *flying leeches*, as they suck your blood and sometimes leave a disease that may kill you, such as malaria and yellow fever.

Mosquitoes may spray saliva onto your skin, then suck your blood with their built-in, six, razor-sharp, tiny needles in their mouths. And it's amazing, no male mosquitoes suck blood, only the females are the Draculas. And usually, of course, mosquitoes attack you in dark places or at night. "There you are!" they might say. But you often don't see them. All you can do when you are attacked is to hit any part of your face, hands, or feet with the palms of both hands. Then blood squirts from their bodies onto your skin!

Mosquitoes populate the world by laying 200 to 300 eggs at a time in ponds or puddles or stagnant water.

Butterflies and Moths. Both bright-colored, butterflies and moths belong to the Lepidoptera order, which means "scaly wings." A butterfly's or a moth's wings are covered with little overlapping scales. While the butterfly's antennae are long and slender, the moth's antennae are thin. When resfing, butterflies usually hold their wings together. On the other hand, moths spread out their wings. In general, butterflies fly during the day, while moths fly at night. However, there are also some moths that are day-fliers.

Butterflies are insects with four wings and six legs. They have two eyes made up of many parts. They also have built-in television antennae which they use for feeling and receiving sound waves for smelling and hearing.

Butterflies are known for their efficient sucking of liquids from flowers with their long, tube-like mouths, which are like vacuum cleaners that suck dirt from the carpet. And their wings move at a rate of 460 to 636 beats a minute.

7. Bugging Bugs and Chewing Beetles

Bugs sometimes bug humans. Bugs belong to the Hemiptera order of insects, which have sucking mouthparts thickened toward the back, such as water bugs or squash bugs. Some of the true bugs are squash bugs, bedbugs, and stink bugs. Some bugs are pests, such as lice, cockroaches, or centipedes—they drink animal blood. Usually, bugs have four wings, but others are wingless. Half of a bug's wing is hard, like a beetle's, but the other half is thin.

Bugs are also known as arthropods. Although they look the same, bugs and beetles belong to different groups. The bugs use their mouthparts to suck up liquid food. The beetles use theirs to chew. The bugs' forewings look like leather; sometimes they are similar to the hind wings. The forewings protect the hind wings. The beetles' hard forewings cover the hind wings.

8. Other Invertebrates

There are invertebrate animals which do not fall under any of the above seven classification groups. They are not amphibians, insects, or mammals, but they are also living things. The following paragraphs will describe them.

Microscopic Animals. The smallest animals are the so-called one-cell animals, such as protozoans. Scientists believe that these animals belong to the *protista*, a different kingdom not associated with plant and animal kingdoms.

The amoeba is the simplest protozoan. It, like other protozoans, reproduces by asexual means; that is, splitting into two pieces like an amoeba being divided into two. The four kinds of protozoa are *ciliates, sporazoans, flagellates*, and *sardones*.

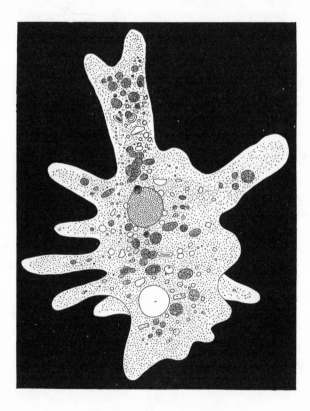

A Species of Amoeba

Some protozoans have their own radars, which are called *eye spots*—bright red spots that are sensitive to light. They move by pushing one part of their cells ahead and then they let the rest follow it. To move, the ciliates use their hairlike projections called *celia*.

Webbing Spiders. The spiders, for instance, are not insects because they have eight legs, not the six legs that insects have. Each of their legs has seven parts. If a spider breaks any part of his body, it can grow a new one. What a wonder!

Of course, there are different kinds of spiders. According to scientists, about 25,000 kinds of them inhabit the Earth.

The spiders are manufacturers—they make silk, and they build webs made of silk. (Some spiders, however, don't web silk.) Actually, the silk is a liquid in their abdomen, but it dries when air touches it. The hub of the wave is made up of "dry" threads; the rest is made up of sticky silk. With this silk, female spiders make sacs in which they lay eggs.

While other insects get stuck in the webs, the spiders don't. Why? Because they have a body-produced oil that covers their bodies. Spiders use webs to capture flies and other insects that get stuck in them, then they finish them off with their sharp fangs that emit a poison, probably similar in some ways to that Saddam Hussein used to spray the Kurds and the Iranians.

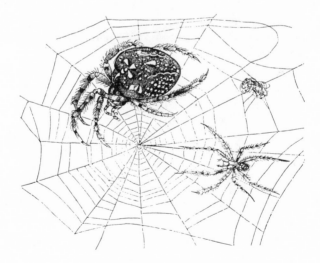

Garden Spiders

Crawling Worms. Worms are legless invertebrate animals with slender, soft bodies. There are several kinds of them, including tapeworms, pink ribbon worms, roundworms, planarians, and segmented worms.

The most common of them are the earthworms, which are soil-eaters and belong to the group of highly developed segmented worms.

Earthworms

The thread-like roundworms, the largest group of them, include the parasitic hookworm.

Planarians are flatworms that abound along the shores of ponds and lakes.

Ribbon worms include the bootlace worm and abound in the ocean.

Pinworms, hookworms, and tapeworms love to live in animal stomachs, where they eat, little by little, its internal parts. In fact, some flatworms, which include tapeworms, enter the stomach and the intestines of human beings. Sometimes, small children sit on the ground without anything under them, enabling some types of worms to enter their bodies. Other worms enter through the skin. Sometimes, children don't wash their hands or don't use spoons or forks when they eat, enabling some types of worms to enter their bodies when they use their hands in eating.

Another kind of segmented worm, which lives in brooks and ponds, is the leech. It has a sucker on each end and loves to drink animal blood, particularly the blood of human beings. So when you or your child wades through a brook or a stream, beware!

Where Animals Live

Many animals live in different places: in the polar regions; in the mountains; on grasslands; in deserts; on the seashores; in streams, ponds, and marshes; in rivers and oceans; and in unusual places such as the insides of animals' bodies or on pools of oil.

For example, frogs, toads, and beavers live in forest ponds and streams; cattle, sheep, and goats live on grasslands; tigers and jaguars live in giant forests; insects and spiders live in the coolest peaks on land; and one-cell protozoans, as well as whales and other animals, live in the oceans.

Some animals, like beavers, build homes of mud and pieces of wood near waterways. Some birds dwell in hollow logs or dead trees. Some animals live in underground homes. In the case of turtles, they bring their own houses wherever they go.

How Animals Move

Animals are defined as living things that move. Of course, not all things that move are animals. Animals move in different ways, such as:

crawling	flying	gliding
hopping	swimming	galloping
jumping	slithering	leaping
walking	diving	running
gliding		

For example, a bird can walk on the ground or fly or glide in the air. A man can walk or run or swim or dive. And whoever said that man couldn't fly?

How Animals Communicate

Animals communicate with each other by sound, body language, taste, odor, touch, or a combination of any or all of these. However, most of them convey sounds.

For instance, the cats may say "Meow, meow"; the pigs, "Oink, oink"; the dogs, "Ggggrrrrllll"; the hyenas, "Ha, ha, ha, ha, ha"; the grasshoppers, "Chirp, chirp, chirp." They make all kinds of sounds to call their mates for food or lovemaking or to alert them of any danger.

How Animals Use Body Parts

Animals have body parts suited to their way of life. For example, the sharp teeth of a beaver is used to cut down trees. The long neck and legs enable a giraffe to reach the top of trees so he can eat leaves. The frog has legs used for hopping and webbed feet used for swimming. The "sonar" of a bat determines its route while flying in the dark, like a Stealth bomber seeing and targeting enemies at night through its night scope.

Also, a fish uses its tail fins to swim and other fins to maneuver and to balance. A snake moves by gripping the ground with its scales and undulating its body in an s-form. A cat extends its retractable claws to climb trees. Animals use different ways to move their bodies to near or far-away places. Like humans, some animals, like fish and birds, migrate to some places during certain times of the year!

Weapons for War

Like humans who have their Patriot and Scud missiles and poison gas, animals have their own weapons, too. They use them to fight their enemies and predators. For example, the cat has claws and teeth to grab and kill its prey, as if saying "I got you!" The hognose snake just lies down motionless as if saying, "I'm dead, you leave me!" The skunk bombards his enemy with a foul-smelling liquid, as if shouting, "Come closer and you're dead!" Yes, animals use different practical or strange things when confronted by their enemies and predators.

But the most effective weapon used by some animals when attacked, especially those who can run fast, such as the deer, is "Run! Run!"—much like a running letter carrier being chased by a pit bulldog.

How Animals Reproduce

Animals reproduce in two ways: *sexual* and *asexual*. *Reproduction* is the process by which an animal or plant creates an organism or thing of its own image or kind. *Regeneration* is the process by which a lost part regrows or an entire new animal grows from a piece of an original living thing. (What a wonder, if only humans could do that!)

Sexual. Humans are familiar with sexual reproduction. It's the thing that makes the heart beat faster. The male sperm and the female egg are the participants in sexual reproduction—they produce something through fertilization.

The two types of fertilization are *internal* and *external.* In internal fertilization, the male releases the sperm that unites with the egg in a female's body. Of course, before this takes place, there should be some kind of attraction or romancing. For instance, the female moth attracts the male by its own scent or perfume. The male frog or grasshopper attracts the female by making love sounds or mating calls. Then the male and the female meet and make love, as if saying, "You're mine and I'm yours!"

In external fertilization, most fish and amphibians shoot their sperm and eggs into the water. Then each sperm hunts his mate as if asking, "Where are you?" and the egg may answer, "Here I am!" Then the two unite to create something. (That's amazing!)

Asexual. *Asexual reproduction* is the process of development without the union of male and female germ cells, such as in budding and fission.

1. **Budding.** *Budding* is the process by which a new thing or individual develops from an outgrowth on the body of a plant or a certain lower animal or living thing.

2. **Fission.** When an animal or plant cell reaches a certain size, it just splits in the middle and forms two small "daughter cells." These daughters, enclosed in separate spheroid cells and each having its own elastic wall, remain together, along with the cells of the plant or the animal in the area of the common outer plant or animal wall. In short, the one cell becomes two, proving the point that in union, there is strength. Scientists call this the simplest form of reproduction. It is *fission.*

In other words, asexual is a kind of reproduction without the participation of two lovers or partners or the "chase-and-catch-me" approach between the sperm and the egg of amphibians. Asexual reproduction takes place in the development of some worms or sponges into new separate things or individuals. A tapeworm, for instance, grows longer. Then it changes into a group of connected individuals. After that, the new individuals declare their independence and separate from the main body to make their own livelihood.

Definition of a Cell

The cell is the smallest and simplest part of living matter, in which the most basic life processes take place, including growth and the release of energy. The parts of a cell are the *cytosol*, the *nucleus*, the *Mitochondria*, and the *endoplasmic reticulum*.

Like Mother,
Like Daughter,
or Not at All!

Some baby animals resemble their parents from birth. But others change their forms or beings as they grow older. For example, actress Meryl Streep delivers a baby that looks like her or her husband.

But in the case of butterflies, it's different. A butterfly lays an egg, and the egg develops into different stages of life to eventually become an adult. This change from embryo to adult is called *metamorphosis*. First, the egg hatches and out comes a caterpillar—this is called the *larva stage*. Then after growing, it sheds its old skin for a new one. Afterwards, it makes silk and with the use of its silk, it fastens itself to a leaf or a twig—this is called the *pupa stage*. Next, some strange things happen inside the hard form called *chrysalis*, which is under the skin. The body then becomes a soft liquid from which legs, wings, and other parts of the body of the butterfly are formed. In the coming of spring, the warm weather wakes up the chrysalis, and then the new butterfly breaks out of its world, as if saying, "I'm coming!"—this is called the *imago* or *adult stage*.

Brief Facts about Animals

■ There are two kinds of animals, the *nocturnal* and the *diurnal.* Nocturnal animals work at night and sleep by day. Diurnal animals work during the day and sleep at night.

■ The noisiest animal is the blue whale. It emits low-frequency sounds of deafening volume—as loud as the sound caused by the engine of a jet taking off.

■ There are three different animals that make silk: the spiders, the moths' silkworms that wrap them up in silk as caterpillars, and the small symphylans related to the centipedes.

■ The bird "song," an auditory signal, is used by birds to attract mates and alert other birds of danger.

■ The grasshoppers make their familiar chirping sound by rubbing their hind legs against the ribs of their fore wings.

■ Crabs don't swim; they use all of their four pairs of legs to move sideways.

■ Some animals hibernate; that is, they sleep underground or elsewhere to escape the snow and the biting cold of winter. During hibernation, their body temperature lowers and their breathing slows down.

The hyenas are any of the w o l f - l i k e carnivorous animals of Africa and Asia that are great hunters. They hunt in groups and communicate by howling screams. But they are known for their laughing—they laugh and scream while hunting. "Ha! Ha! Ha! Ha! Ha!" they say. That's why they have been nicknamed "laughing hyenas."

A Striped Hyena

Wild and Tame Animals

Many animals abound in forests, but other animals are tamed by man. Some of the tame animals have become pets or have been put in zoos for experiment or entertainment. In the home, we have cats and dogs. In aquariums, tropical fish. In zoos, monkeys, tigers, and lions. In the entertainment world, such as in Marineland, dolphins and other animals.

Endangered Species

Many nations are taking steps to preserve some animals— the so-called endangered species. Those are animals that are dwindling in population, some being very few in numbers. Without protection, they are near extinction. Dinosaurs and other giant animals have been extinct for eons.

Some animals in danger of becoming extinct are koala bears, white whales, blue whales, rhinoceroses, African elephants, ocelots, platypuses, and Tasmanian tigers (related to kangaroos and koala bears).

How to Teach about Animals

When you teach your child about animals, let him go with you to the fish store to see unusual and tropical fish in aquariums; to the zoo to witness how tigers, lions, monkeys, and other animals move and play; and to museums to learn things about extinct and endangered species of animals.

Conclusion

Some animals are useful to us; they give us food, entertainment, or companionship. But others can be harmful—those that can harm, kill, or eat us if they have the opportunity to do so.

But whether friends or enemies, they are our neighbors on Planet Earth. How we deal and associate with them is up to us.

That's why it's important for our children to study how they move and live. Like us, they're interesting creatures.

How Plants Live **15**

Plants grow on land, in fresh or salt water, and above the ground. It is estimated that there are over 335,000 kinds of plants. They have different sizes, shapes, and colors—from tiny algae to fungi to giant trees that can grow as tall as 300 feet.

As mentioned in chapter 14, plants and animals are classified into the major groups of *kingdom, phylum, class, order, family, tribe, genus,* and *species.*

For the subject areas studied at different grade levels, see those discussed on those pages 138 – 141.

I. The Plant Kingdom

The plant kingdom is divided into the following four divisions:

■ **Thallophyta.** This is composed of algae, bacteria, blue-green algae, and fungi.

■ **Bryophyta.** Belonging to this division are mosses and liverworts.

■ **Pteridophyta.** Included in this division are ferns, horsetails, and club mosses.

■ **Spermatophyta.** This division consists of gymnosperms (coniferous trees) and angiosperms (flowering plants).

1. Thallophyta

Algae, bacteria, blue-green algae, and fungi belong to organisms called *prokaryotes.* Since they don't have specialized structures or organelles, which are usually present in plants, many scientists consider them as a separate kingdom. Since they have no chlorophyll, they can't process their own food and are dependent on other living things—plants and animals, dead or alive.

a. Bacteria. Bacteria are microscopic living cells that cause things to decay. Although harmful to humans because they cause diseases, they are considered helpful in their own way—if it were not for them, dead things and junks would continue to pile up and cover the Earth.

b. *Algae.* The simplest form of plants, algae can't manufacture their own food and they depend on water for their livelihood. In fact, they don't even have roots, stems, leaves, or water-conducting tissues. Algae are distinguishable according to their colors, with brown being the dominant color. Brown algae consist of almost all the seaweeds. When you treat these seaweeds with hot water, they become green.

c. *Fungi.* Fungi are considered plants, but they are different from other plants in the sense that they don't have chlorophyll—the green color in plant leaves. Since they also have no ability to manufacture their own food, they depend on other living or nonliving things for their nourishment.

The three groups of fungi are *phycomycetes, ascomycetes,* and *basidiomycetes.* They differ in characteristics in the following manner: the *phycomycetes* have free-swimming *zoospores;* the *ascomycetes* have cells with cross-walls that can produce eight spores in special arrangements, called *asci,* with floating bodies. Examples of phycomycetes are water molds like green algae and mushrooms, which are the most advanced group of fungi. Examples of ascomycetes are yeast (*sacharomyces*) and *penicillium notatum,* the producer of penicillin. Examples of basidiomycetes are poisonous mushrooms, which are called *toadstools.*

2. Bryophyta

Bryophyta, composed of mosses and liverworts, are the simplest of land plants.

a. **Mosses.** Mosses, numbering about 14,000 species, are any of various classes of very small, green bryophytes with stems that have leaf-like structures. They grow in clusters on trees, rocks, and moist ground.

b. **Liverworts.** Liver-shaped, liverworts are any of two classes (hepaticopsida and anthocenotopsida) of bryophytes that form dense, green moss-like mats on logs, rocks, or moist ground. There are about 9,000 species of liverworts.

3. Pteridophyta

a. **Ferns.** These nonflowering embryophytes with roots, stems, and fronds reproduce not by seeds, but by spores. Spores are reproduction bodies that usually consist of a single cell, and they are produced by bacteria, algae, mosses, ferns, and certain protozoans. They are produced both asexually and sexually by the union of gametes. Tree ferns are the largest ferns.

b. **Horsetails.** Horsetails are any of the only surviving genus (equisetophyta) of plants having hollow, jointed stems. Horsetails have scale-like leaves at the joints and have spores borne in cones.

c. **Club Mosses.** Club mosses are any of a division of fossils or living vascular plants with small leaves. They have a single vascular strand, and spores are produced in cones at the tip of the stem or in leaf axils.

4. Spermatophyta

Spermatophyta are of two kinds: *gymnosperms* and *angiosperms*.

a. **Gymnosperms.** In these coniferous trees, secondary growth is common, allowing the formation of trees like pine and spruce. The oldest of living plants which produce true seeds, gymnosperms' male gametophyte is confined to a nucleus in small, windborne spores (pollen). Today's gymnosperms are woody trees with evergreen foliage. One of them is the fir tree.

b. **Angiosperms.** These flowering plants are divided into two subphyla: *dicotyledonae*, which contain two seed leaves with branching leaf veins (cotyledons), and *monocotyledonae*, which contain one seed leaf (long, narrow leaves with parallel veins) and which include all grasses and cereals. An example of the cotyledonae trees is the plane tree, while an example of the monocotyledonae is the palm tree. The classification of angiosperms is based on the structure of seeds and fruits.

II. How Plants Reproduce

Plants, like animals, reproduce in two ways: *sexual* and *asexual* reproduction.

Sexual Reproduction. Sexual reproduction involves the action of both male and female sex organs of plants and animals.

1. **Pollination.** *Pollination* is the process by which pollen grains are transported from a stamen or a microphosporophyl to a stigma or an ovule. Pollens are carried by wind, water, and certain animals, such as insects, some birds (such as hummingbirds, honeysuckers, and honey eaters), and some bats.

Plants need pollinators so that their flowers can be pollinated. Animals need flowers for their nectar and pollen. Some insects lay eggs in flowers whose parts are eaten by larvae— some of these larvae are, of course, eaten by birds and bats.

a. *Wind Pollination.* In the case of trees, many of them are separate male and female plants. They have separate productive organs borne in cones called *strobili.* Male cones produce a great number of tiny pollen. When the wind blows, pollen is transferred onto the cones of female plants, then the eggs are fertilized. And they're probably saying, "I want to mate! I want to mate!" And the union is made.

b. *Animal Pollinators.* In the case of flowering plants, a sugary substance is produced by flowers in glands on the petals, called *nectaries.* When pollinators such as insects or birds seek nectar and pollen, their bodies are covered with the pollen produced by the male sex organ (anthers). When they go from flower to flower to get nectar, the pollinators may leave some of the pollen on the female sex organ (stigma). Then the eggs are fertilized.

When the pollen is transferred from the male sex organ to the female sex organ of the same plant, it's called *self-pollination.* When the pollen of a flower is deposited into the female sex organ of another flower, it's called *cross-pollination.* The pollinators are attracted by the plant's colors and smell. "Come and kiss me!" some flowers might be shouting. Then the pollinators, whether a bird, an insect, or a bat, goes to the newly found mate and says, "Give me food, darling, and here's what you need!" And they continue such an activity day by day, week by week, and year by year!

2. **Spores.** *Spores* are any of various reproduction bodies produced by certain plants instead of seeds. They usually consist of a single cell, produced by bacteria, algae, mosses, ferns, and certain protozoans. They are produced either sexually, by the union of *gametes* (sexual spores) or asexually (asexual spores). In some plants, ferns for instance, within a single layer of sterile epidermal cells is a spore case carrying a single group of spores.

These spores are liberated as a result of the rupture of the epidermal covering and new things come from the spores, which are called *gametophytes.* Below the gametophytes, next to the moist soil, develop two types of sex organs, male and female. The sperm, which are relatively small, are produced on the basis of the nutritive capital of a young gametophyte.

The male sex organs of a certain gametophyte usually discharge their sperm before the female sex organs of the same gametophyte are ready to receive them. In this case, the eggs of the latter can be fertilized only by the sperm of another gametophyte in the nearby areas.

3. **Breeding.** In the case of aims to increase the yield of some plants (flowers or seeds, for instance, and particularly the cereals), man cross-breeds plants, which is called *breeding.* Man sterilizes the maturation or the function of certain male sex organs (stamens) and uses the other male sex organs.

In other words, the production of hybrid seed between two strains is accomplished by interplanting a sterile version of one strain (say A) in an isolated field with a fertile version of another strain. Hence, a new improved seed, fruit, or plant is produced. It's just like the breeding of animals: A hybrid animal makes love with a female to produce a hybrid offspring. It's just like the marrying of two individuals of different races to produce a human being of neither race.

Asexual Reproduction. As mentioned in chapter 14, asexual reproduction means the reproduction of animals and plants not done by the union of sperm and eggs. It is accomplished through budding or fission, which is common among lower forms of animals and plants.

1. **Budding** (see page 161).

2. **Fission** (see page 161).

3. **Spores.** As mentioned above, spores can also be produced asexually, without the union of sperm and eggs.

How Plants Grow

Like animals, plants have their own growth hormones. Different plant hormones, or growth regulators, have different effects on plant growth. The best known hormones are the *auxins*. Auxins are formed in young, growing organs, such as opening buds, to different parts of the body to stimulate the cells to elongate and sometimes to divide. Then the plant grows and expands.

III. How Plants Manufacture Food

As humans, we can't manufacture food inside our bodies; we are parasites. We depend on animals and plants for food, which we then cook or prepare in different ways. But plants manufacture their own food; they have their own factories in their own bodies.

The roots are the plants' mouths, transporting water and other dissolved mineral nutrients from the ground to the leaves, where they are processed as food, mostly sugar for distribution to other parts, such as reproductive organs—the flowers and the fruits. A plant has its own blood vessels criss-crossing all over its body. The blood vessels in the forms of narrow strands are divided into two kinds: the *xylem* and the *phloem*. The so-called *vascular plants,* such as trees, have well-developed xylem and phloem; some plants have less-developed xylem and phloem. Other plants, which don't have these plant tissues are called *nonvascular plants.*

The Xylem. This structure consists of tiny long tubes in the stem, called *vessels,* through which water and other nutrients ascend into all plant parts, primarily into the leaves, where they are cooked or processed as food through a process known as *photosynthesis.* Photosynthesis is the process by which carbohydrate food is transformed from carbon dioxide and water in the presence of chlorophyll, using light energy and releasing oxygen. (In certain bacteria, photosynthesis occurs with the involvement of pigments other than chlorophyll.)

The Phloem. A phloem consists of two kinds of living cells, *sieve tube cells* and *companion cells.* Its main function is to transport processed carbohydrates from the leaves down to all parts of the plant. "Here's the food," the leaves say as they send the processed food to the other parts of the body.

The Cambium. Between the xylem and the phloem, a few layers of narrow cells, called *cambium*, abound. The cell stems of big trees, such as flowering plants with two seed leaves (such as oaks, elms, and maples) reproduce new cells, replacing aging xylem and phloem cells. This results in the increase in diameter of the stem with each season's secondary growth. Then the xylem is formed as a woody cylinder on the inner side of the cambium layer near the stem's center. The cambium deposits the tissues (xylem) as a complex network to be sure that the flow of water inside the plant's body is never interrupted, even though the stem is injured, causing damage to some tissues.

Moreover, the amounts of xylem layers formed every year become rings, popularly known as *annual rings*. They are visible in the cross-sections of stems. Of course, the oldest rings are those in the heartwood—the dead central core. The central core has a darker color, while the lighter sapwood is alive and functions as storage tissue and conducting tissue—where processed food passes through. Meanwhile, the younger annual rings comprise the sapwood. Through these rings, we can tell how old a tree is—each ring is one year.

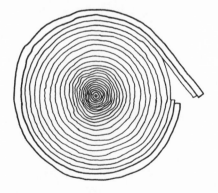

Each Ring Represents One Year

On the other hand, the secondary phloem is produced toward the outside of the stem from the cambium layer, creating the inner, conducting bark. The phloem layer, which is very thin—less than .5 millimeter—is renewed every year. The older phloem serves as food storage, while the new phloem acts as the conducting tissues. Now the storing and conducting phloem become the living bark. Of course, the oldest phloem layers are outermost most, which are the dead bark of the stem surface.

The Leaves. As already mentioned, food is processed in the leaves through photosynthesis. But the leaves have also other jobs. There are special structures in the leaves, called *stomata*, which contain pores whose openings are managed by a flexible part of cells called *guard cells*. The guard cells see to it that the pores are open during the day and closed during the night. The pores should be open so that water vapor can escape from the plant and so that carbon dioxide can come in to participate in photosynthesis—the processing of food. At night, the guard cells might be shouting, "Close the doors! Close the doors!" They are doing that so there won't be an excessive loss of water. So the stomata are closed. So you see, plant parts act as parts of humans do!

Teaching Your Child about Plants

You should teach your child the following:

The parts of plants are roots, stems, leaves, flowers, and fruits. (In the case of trees, the trunk is the stem.) Their duties are as follows:

1. Roots: to bring water and minerals from the soil to the leaves for processing as food for the whole plant.

2. Stem: to hold the plant up so it won't fall.

3. Leaves: to process water and minerals into sugar, with the aid of light energy and chlorophyll, the green pigments in the leaves. Leaves also have openings to inhale carbon dioxide, the air we expel, and to exhale oxygen, the air we breathe.

4. Flowers: to produce fruits and seeds for new plants.

5. Fruits: the products that animals eat.

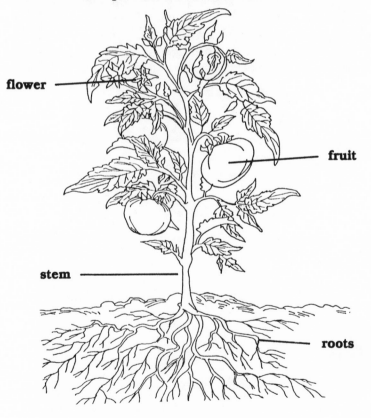

Parts of a Plant

■ Most plants begin from seeds. However, other plants begin from roots, tubers, or stems. Some start from spores, tiny bodies that are produced sexually and asexually as explained in the early part of this chapter.

■ Plants need soil, air, sunshine, and water for growth.

■ Cereal is made from grains of rice, corn, or wheat. Bread is made from grains.

■ There are different kinds of plants. For the layman, the most known plants are herbs, shrubs, vines, flowering plants, ferns, and trees. In the case of trees, there are two kinds: *dediduous*, which lose their leaves in the fall, and *evergreen*, which keep their leaves all year 'round. Plants, especially those known as vascular plants, have tissue vessels, such as the xylem and the phloem. The xylem transports water and dissolved minerals from the roots to the leaves for processing as food. The phloem moves the processed food, mostly sugar, from the leaves to all parts of the plant for growth. Between the xylem and the phloem is the cambium, a network of cells capable of reproducing new cells, replacing old xylem and phloem cells.

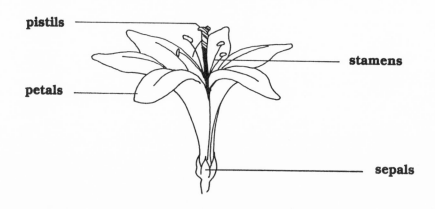

Parts of a Flower

■ Vines are not parasites. They cling to other plants and things for support.

■ Seeds travel or are scattered on the ground through the following methods:

1. Seeds pop from their location in trees.

2. Some seeds stick to animals' fur and are carried away.

3. Birds drop seeds after eating fruits.

4. Man buries seeds in the ground to make them grow.

■ Fruit- and vegetable-producing plants grow under the ground (such as root crops) and above the ground (such as corn and tomatoes).

■ Some plants live only a few weeks. Others live for a long time.

■ Plant leaves change color. When the weather turns cooler, the tree is no longer capable of sending much water from the roots to the leaves. With less light, or none at all, the chlorophyll in the leaves begins to fade so the true colors of the leaves—red, orange, or yellow—appear. When fall comes, a special chemical that connects the leaf to the twig breaks down; then the leaves stop their photosynthesis—the processing of food. Afterwards, the leaves become dead and fall. It's fall!

Uses of Plants

Plants are important to man. They give us flowers, decoration, and wood. Wood is transformed into many products, including paper and lumber. From plants, we also get dyes, medicines, cotton, gum, rubber, etc.

There's an endless list of what plants give us. But one important thing is oxygen. In turn, we give them what we expel, carbon dioxide. Thus, they clean the air that we breathe. So you see, our lives are interrelated. That's why we, especially in this time of the so-called warming of the Earth, are urged to plant more trees. That's why, too, you need to explain to your child how plants grow and why plants are important to us.

Earth and Space 16

More than ever before, the past few years have been witnessed by man as the Age of Space Exploration. Through space vehicles and modern technology, Americans and Soviets have probed Earth and space with vigor, courage, and determination.

At the same time, we have been awakened by the so-called "warming of the Earth."

These developments have added interest and enthusiasm among education authorities and teachers in teaching resources of the Earth and how space and weather affect our daily lives.

★ ★ ★ ★ ★

I. Subject Areas

Generally, the subject areas taught in the majority of elementary schools in the country are as described in the following paragraphs.

★ ★ ★ ★ ★

Kindergarten

In kindergarten, the study of rocks, land, and water is already taught. In view of this, ensure that your child knows how to collect and manipulate different kinds of rocks. He must also know how to classify little or large and rough or smooth rocks.

The study of the Sun and the Moon and the different seasons is introduced in kindergarten. For instance, your child should be able to identify pictures of astronauts and to imagine space travel.

★ ★ ★ ★ ★
Grade 1

In this grade, your child should already be familiar with the space around the Earth and the shapes of the Sun, the stars, and the clouds. By this time, he should be able to name the different planets from memory.

Also, he should already know how to locate and identify rocks and rock formations around his community.

★ ★ ★ ★ ★
Grade 2

At this grade level, familiarize your child with the Sun and the Earth's air and water, the weather changes, and the phases of the Moon. He should also continue the study of rocks.

He should also know how to define the properties and the uses of air and water and to name the different types of clouds.

★ ★ ★ ★ ★
Grade 3

The size, the distance, the motion, and the phases of the Sun, the Moon, and other planets are taught in this grade.

Your child must be familiar with what the Earth's resources are and how the Earth changes as years pass. At this grade level, he should already know the so-called water cycle.

The knowledge of how rocks are formed and how rocks are affected by wind and water erosion is a must for your child.

★ ★ ★ ★ ★

Grade 4

At this grade level, the teaching of the characteristics of the Solar System is a must. The study of rocks should be continued. Other minerals should also be studied. Moreover, the study of the Earth's oceans and its resources is taught at this grade level.

By this time, your child should already know how to measure weather through various instruments, such as a thermometer.

★ ★ ★ ★ ★

Grade 5

Grade 5 students are taught of other things in space beyond the Solar System. Changes in the weather, particularly those that involve air pressure and winds, and air masses and clouds, are taught in this grade. In view of this, review these things with your child.

★ ★ ★ ★ ★

Grade 6

The exploration of space is fully studied in this grade. So familiarize him with the American and Soviet exploration programs.

Be sure that he knows fully well the Earth's resources, how the Earth's underground plates move, and how to forecast the weather.

Regarding the seasons, teach your child how people, animals, and plants are affected by seasonal changes—for instance, from summer to fall, from fall to winter, and from winter to spring.

* ★ ★ ★ ★ ★

II. The Solar System

The Sun, the Earth, the Moon, and the eight other planets compose the *Solar System*. Those planets are Mercury, Venus, Mars, Jupiter, Saturn, Neptune, Uranus, and Pluto.

The Solar System, in which the Earth belongs, is only a tiny part of a galaxy which includes millions of stars. This galaxy is known as the *Milky Way*. These space bodies are held together by the force of gravity as the galaxy travels in space. However, there are other galaxies in the vast space beyond the Milky Way.

The Sun

The Sun is a giant nuclear furnace. It's really a star—only one of billions of stars in space. However, it is the nearest star to the Earth, a distance of 93,000,000 miles. It's the Earth's source of light and heat energy. Were it not for the Sun's energy, human beings, animals, and plants would be extinct. Of course, the Moon gives us light at night, too; but its light is a reflected light from the Sun.

The Sun is a ball of burning gases whose surface temperature is about 10,000 degrees Fahrenheit and whose deep inside temperature is about 25,000,000 degrees Fahrenheit. Its gases, consisting of at least 60 other elements, are mostly hydrogen and helium. Hydrogen acts as the Sun's main fuel; it changes into helium that releases great amounts of energy. This process is known as *nuclear fusion*.

There will come a time that the Sun's hydrogen will all be consumed—resulting in its death. However, don't worry about it. It will be millions of years from now.

The Sun is divided into four parts: the *core* (the center), the *radiative zone*, the *convective zone*, and the *photosphere*. The core is the Sun's factory; it is where heat and light are produced. The photosphere that radiates sunshine to Earth is the outside part of the Sun. The Earth and all the other planets that revolve around the Sun are affected by its gravitational force. Of course, you may wonder why the Sun doesn't grab the Earth and swallow it! (I'm wondering, too!) The Earth completes circling the Sun in 365 days, a year.

Mercury

The nearest planet to the Sun is Mercury, about 36,000,000 miles away. The fastest of all the planets, Mercury makes a complete orbit around the Sun every 3 months, as compared to the Earth's year.

If you could stand on Mercury, you would see there is no water or life there—it is covered with dust. You would also see many craters filled with lava—lava that might have been produced by erupting volcanoes and by molten rocks caused by meteorites that crashed on the planet.

Venus

The slowest of the planets, Venus is the second planet closest to the Sun, a distance of 67,000,000 miles away.

Almost the same size as the Earth, Venus shines brightly at night, so bright that it is probably next to the Moon's brightness. It completes the orbit around the Sun in 225 days.

Venus has attracted both Americans and Soviets. In fact, it has been explored by 23 space vehicles, including 5 robot explorers from the United States and 18 from the Soviet Union. These spacecraft took pictures of the planet, including its clouds. Several vehicles landed on the planet, but all the robot space vehicles became inoperative due to the planet's hostile environment.

Earth

Known as the *Blue Planet*, the Earth is the only planet with water. In fact, water occupies 70 percent of its surface. About 93,000,000 miles from the Sun, it weighs about 6,600 million trillion tons.

The Earth is a large magnet. Buildings, water, humans, animals, and plants are pulled by a powerful force to prevent them from falling into space. That's why anything you throw into the air always comes down. This force is called *gravity.*

Long, long years ago, people believed that the Earth was flat. Then it was discovered that it was round—meaning that if a ship traveled east, it would, in due time, reach west. But actually, the Earth is not perfectly round; it bulges slightly at the Equator.

In 1968, the Earth was seen as a planet by peoples of different nations as if hanging in space—like a balloon suspended in air. "Oh! So that's the Earth!" many people might have said. That's when Apollo 8 astronauts Frank Gorman, James A. Lovell, Jr., and William A. Anders circled the Moon and photographed the Earth rising above the lunar horizon. The picture showed a fantastic blue and white ball—the blue caused by the oceans' waters and the white by the clouds.

The Parts of the Earth. The Earth is divided into three parts: the *core*, about 2,170 miles in thickness; the *mantle*, about 8,800 miles in thickness; and the *crust*, about 22 miles in thickness.

Of course, the core, the center of the Earth, is believed to be made of iron and nickel. The mantle is made of hot, dense rock. The crust, covered by seas, is believed to be made of lightweight rocks, including granite and basalt.

The Drifting Continents. It is believed that millions of years ago, there was only one large, solid land surrounded by water. South America was then connected to Africa. This theory is supported by the fact that rocks, about 150 million years old, found near the coasts of these continents were of the same kind. However, in other parts of the Atlantic Ocean, rocks were found to be younger in age. In view of this, scientists theorized that all the continents were once joined.

Called *Pangae*, which means "all land," the supercontinent was believed to have broken up into sections by force of nature into what looks something like today's continents. As of now, we have seven continents: Europe, Asia, Africa, Australia, North America, South America, and Antarctica. These continents are surrounded by the Atlantic, Pacific, and Indian oceans. But since these continents are standing on huge slabs of rock, there are some movements occurring day by day, week by week. As one huge rock slab pushes into or rides over another rock, earthquakes occur. Volcanic eruptions and mountain building also make these slabs of rock move.

It is believed that millions of years from now, the continents will once again be connected to each other.

The Moon. The Earth has one orbiting moon. American astronauts first landed on the Moon in July 1969. It was then that Apollo 11 Commander Neil Armstrong stepped from his lunar landing craft as more than a billion people watch on television. Thus, he became the first human to set foot in another world. When they left the Moon, they left behind a plaque signed by President Richard M. Nixon, which read, "Here men from planet Earth first set foot upon the Moon—July 1969 A.D.—We came in Peace for all Mankind."

Since then, six manned Apollo landings found the Moon to have no water, no air, and no living things. Since there's neither water nor air, there's no weather, tornadoes, hurricanes, or earthquakes on the Moon. The Moon contains dust, igneous rocks, and craters. The only things that change the Moon's surface are the so-called *micrometeorites* that bombard it at speeds of up to 70,000 miles per hour. These micrometeorite landings cause some craters and the lunar soil, a layer of powder and rubble, to form 3 to 60 feet deep.

(More details on the Earth and weather are on pages 185 – 192.)

Mars

For years, it was believed that there were more-advanced living creatures on Mars, called *Martians.* In fact, on Halloween eve, 1938, a CBS radio program was interrupted by a newscast that announced that Earth was being invaded by Martians. Over six million people heard Orson Welles's "Mercury Theater" that reported the landings of Martians in Grover's Mill in New Jersey, Buffalo, Chicago, St. Louis, and in several places in Virginia. Excited reporters shouted: "The Martians have landed! The Martians have landed!" Many people panicked, men prepared for battle, while women and children ran for cover, cried, and prayed. It was the war of the worlds, they thought. It turned out later that the one-hour news program was part of a dramatic story based on the story *The War of the Worlds.*

Mars, the so-called *Red Planet* because the rusted iron in the soil makes the crater-filled planet look red, is the fourth major planet from the Sun and is closest to the Earth. It is

142,000,000 miles from the Sun. Most of the air on Mars is 95 percent carbon dioxide. It's covered with large deserts and enveloped with wild dust storms in the summer. It has neither oceans nor lakes. Like on Earth, the day on Mars is about 24 hours.

Mars completes its orbit of the Sun in 687 Earth days. It looks like a bright star when viewed from the Earth. Two moons orbit the planet—Phobos, the inner moon, and Deimos, the outer moon.

Robot space vehicles have already explored Mars. The first one to fly by it was Mariner 4 in 1965. The second and third were Mariners 6 and 7 in 1969. Others followed. Vikings 1 and 2 landed there in 1976 and took pictures of the planet's surface. But they found no living organisms.

Jupiter

Known as the *Giant Planet,* Jupiter is the fifth planet from the Sun, about 484,000,000 miles away. Made mostly of hydrogen with some helium, the diameter at its Equator is 89,000 miles. It orbits the Sun in 11.9 years and spins on its axis in 9 hours, 56 minutes.

Gases such as methane, ammonia, and water vapor occupy the clouds around Jupiter. Tiny particles and large rocks form a ring that extends some 34,000 miles to encircle the planet.

Jupiter reflects more sunlight than any other planet, except Venus. It has four moons.

Saturn

Saturn, the sixth planet from the Sun, is the second largest planet in the Solar System.

Like Jupiter, Saturn is a huge, spinning, gaseous body consisting mostly of hydrogen and helium. Strong winds blow the thick layers of clouds covering the planet.

During a voyage years ago, Voyager 1, an American unmanned spacecraft, took photographs of swirling rock, ice and dust that comprise Saturn's rings.

Saturn has 17 known moons, the largest of which is Titan, the second largest known moon in the entire Solar System.

Uranus

The seventh planet from the Sun, Uranus is 32,200 miles in diameter at its Equator and orbits the Sun in 84 years. Uranus has ten thin, dark rings—all consisting primarily of boulder-sized chunks of dark matter.

Fifteen moons are known to be orbiting Uranus. The largest are Miranda, Ariel, Umbriel, Titania, and Oberon. In 1986, Voyager 2 took photographs of Uranus' moons.

Neptune

The eighth planet from the Sun, Neptune has a diameter of 30,800 miles at its Equator. Under the outer atmosphere are layers of gases and liquids, mostly hydrogen. A layer of ice and a core of rock and iron are believed to be contained inside.

Neptune, with at least three rings, has eight known moons. Triton, one of the moons, is larger than the Earth's Moon and orbits Neptune in six of our days.

Pluto

Pluto, the smallest of the planets and the ninth from the Sun, was the last planet to be discovered by astronomers. With an estimated diameter at its Equator of only 1,800 miles, Pluto orbits the Sun in 248 years. Its spins on its axis in 6 days, 9 hours.

Pluto is covered with methane ice that reflects sunlight very well. Rocks, frozen methane, and water are believed by scientists to be inside Pluto.

Other Matters in Space

Different small bodies also travel in outer space. Some of them are as follows:

Asteroids. Considered as minor planets, asteroids also orbit the Sun. Some 3,000 asteroids, the largest of which is Ceres, revolve around the Sun. They are said to be clumps of material that didn't grow large enough to become a planet. Through a telescope, asteroids look like stars. The word "asteroid" means "like a star."

Comets. "Oh, my God! There's the signal!" people of many years ago used to say when they saw strange things streaking through the sky. They believed that such things, later known as comets, were bad omens of coming wars, famines, and other disasters. Now it is believed that their coming has nothing to do with people's fates. They are just part of the Solar System. Billions of comets are believed to have orbited the Sun. When a comet is far from the Sun, it is a ball of frozen water and frozen gases ("snow") and solids ("dirt").

Believed to have a nucleus, called *coma,* which may stretch out for 60,000 miles, a comet contains dust that reflects sunlight and gases. A tail or two may be millions of miles long.

Meteors. It's not a Patriot! It's not a Scud! It's a meteor!

A meteor is a chunk of stone or metal that plunges into the Earth's atmosphere and then burns. If it doesn't explode and land on the ground, it is called a *meteorite.* When such meteorites crash on the Earth, they create huge craters and are known as *shooting stars.*

★ ★ ★ ★ ★

III. The Earth and the Weather

The Earth's Atmosphere

"Space is infinite!" you may say whenever you look towards the space high above in the sky. Yes, beyond the Earth's atmosphere lies the endless outer space.

Atmosphere. The Earth's atmosphere extends upward to several hundred miles. It protects human beings from excesive heat from the Sun during the day and from too much coldness at night. The atmosphere contains a thin layer of gases which are held closer to the Earth by its gravitational force. The gases include oxygen, the air we breathe. It is divided into five layers (from the ground up), which are as follows:

1. **Troposphere.** Extends upward to 10.5 miles. This layer contains oxygen and all kinds of weather.

2. **Stratosphere.** Extends upward from 10.5 miles to 31 miles. It contains most of the atmosphere's ozone, which absorbs harmful ultraviolet radiation from the Sun. Scientists have discovered that there is a hole in the ozone layer above

Antarctica. They believe that this indicates that air pollution, especially the release of certain chemicals, is damaging the ozone layer.

3. **Mesosphere.** Extends upward from 31 miles to 53 miles.

4. **Thermosphere.** Extends upward from 53 to 310 miles. It is also known as the *ionosphere,* which is the start of outer space. Because electrical particles are contained in it, we may hear something like this, "This is Radio Baghdad!" or "This is Khadafy speaking." The reason is that these electrical particles move radio waves from broadcasting stations to receiving stations.

5. **Exosphere.** Extends upward from 310 miles.

Clouds. Tiny water droplets in the air (that evaporate from water in plants, lakes, rivers, and seas) make clouds. Clouds are formed when the air containing water vapor rises and expands. In other words, they are a mass of tiny, condensed water droplets or ice crystals suspended in the sky. There are many kinds of clouds. Four of them are as follows:

1. **Cirrus.** The highest in the sky, cirrus clouds are nearly straight or irregularly curved fine white filaments and consist of ice crystals.

2. **Cumulus.** Found at low altitudes, cumulus are thin sheets of clouds during calm weather. However, when weather conditions are bad, these bloated clouds cover a large part of the atmosphere. Most of the time, they develop vertically, with a dark, flat base. These clouds bring showers, hail, and thunderstorms.

3. **Stratus.** These low, extensive sheets of gray clouds consist of water droplets and sometimes ice crystals. They usually cause rain drizzles.

4. **Fog.** The term fog refers to a cloud of water vapor condensed to fine particles near the surface of the Earth. It is formed by the condensation of water on the so-called *condensation nuclei* that are present in natural air.

cirrus   **cumulus**

stratus   **fog**

Kinds of Clouds

Warming of the Earth. Carbon dioxide accumulates in the ozone layer, which blocks out deadly ultraviolet rays from the Sun. Scientists have theorized that due to the accumulation of this gas, the heat that the Earth didn't absorb can't escape into outer space. This results in the so-called warming of the Earth theory. This carbon dioxide should be consumed by plants on Earth. But as of now, plants are dwindling.

The Moon Phases

"I'll give you the Moon," a lover might promise a loved one. Yes, the Moon has been the subject of poets, of lovers, and of many people who dream of their bright future to come.

The Moon is the Earth's only satellite. As it orbits the Earth, it gets reflected light from the Sun. At first, the Moon gives just a little light at night, then a little more, until it is radiant with light.

The Moon's phases are divided into *new moon, crescent moon, quarter moon, gibbous moon,* and *full moon.* During the first stage, the appearance of a new moon, it can barely be seen, for it gives only a small light. In the second stage, the crescent moon, the lighted part of the Moon is shaped like a banana. In the third stage, the quarter moon, half of it reflects light. In the fourth stage, the gibbous moon, about two thirds of it is light. In the fifth stage, the full moon, the whole moon reflects light.

Night and Day

We have night and day because when the Earth orbits the Sun, it spins on its axis every 23 hours, 56 minutes, 4 seconds—or about every 24 hours. Of course, the Sun shines all the time and reflects its light to the part of the Earth that faces it. At that time, it's day on that part of the Earth and night on the part facing the opposite direction. For instance, when it's midnight in the Philippines, it's noon in the United States.

The Causes of Eclipses

When the Earth covers the Moon and our World's shadow falls on it, the Moon cannot get light from the Sun, so we can't see the Moon. That is called an *eclipse of the Moon.*

However, when the Moon's shadow covers parts of the Earth, people on that part of our World can't see a lighted Sun. That is called an *eclipse of the Sun.*

The Water Cycle

The hot Sun warms the Earth. Such temperature changes some water in plants, streams, rivers, or seas into water vapor. Warm air is lighter than cool air, so it rises, with the warm air carrying water vapor (gas) into the atmosphere. This process is known as *evaporation*. Afterwards, the rising air cools, and some water vapor condenses into water droplets (liquid) which combine to form clouds. This process is known as *condensation*.

Clouds can have different volumes of water droplets in them. When the tiny water droplets mass together, they become larger and heavier. Then the clouds can no longer hold such a volume of water and the water droplets fall as rain. If it is very cold (as in winter), the water droplets freeze and fall as snow or hail. Rain, snow, and hail are all parts of the process known as *precipitation*. Then the raindrops fill lakes, rivers, and seas.

Afterwards, the hot Sun evaporates some of the water into water vapor and the cycle, from evaporation to condensation to precipitation, repeats itself. This total process is called the *water cycle*.

Summer or Winter?

In the United States and many other parts of the world, there are four seasons: *spring, summer, fall,* and *winter.*

We have these seasons because the Earth is tilted on its axis (the imaginary line which passes through the North and South poles) as it orbits the Sun. For instance, the part of the Earth that is tilted towards the Sun is warm and experiences summer; the part tilted away from the Sun is cool and experiences winter. Of course, the changes of seasons are affected by different patterns of winds and temperatures.

In polar latitudes, the seasons consist of a short summer and a long winter. This division is based solely on sunlight, as there is continuous darkness all winter and continuous daylight or twilight all summer.

In low latitudes, such as in the Philippines, seasonal weather variations are based largely on rainy and dry periods. These changes result from the movements of the so-called *intertropi-*

cal convergence zone, a thin belt of abundant precipitation that encircles the Earth near the Equator. The Sun causes the areas it crosses to have alternating wet and dry seasons. However, those regions near the Equator that are crossed twice each year by the "belt" have two wet and two dry seasons.

The Rainbows

When sunlight hits raindrops, it splits into all the colors of light—red, orange, yellow, green, blue, and violet. As this happens, a rainbow is formed in the sky.

The Geysers

Hot volcanic rocks near the surface of the Earth heat water. If the water becomes hot and turns to steam, it pushes itself upward to create a geyser. An example of such a geyser is Old Faithful in Yellowstone National Park in Wyoming.

The Glaciers

During winter, too much snow falls in such places as polar regions and high mountains; in the summer, not all the snow melts and evaporates.

In other words, glaciers are formed by snow and ice that don't melt but stay on high mountaintops.

However, the icy mass may move slowly downhill, seeking low places. Some of those blocks of ice may break away and eventually melt; some may reach the ocean, where they break off and form floating icebergs.

The Atmosphere and the Weather

The Earth is covered by thin layers of gases, including oxygen, called the *atmosphere.* Gravity holds these gases near the surface of the Earth.

Due to temperature changes, the air across the surface of the Earth moves. When the air blows, it is called the *wind.*

The air is a mixture of gases comprising the Earth's atmosphere. Such gases include nitrogen (about 78.084 percent, oxygen (about 20.946 percent), argon, neon, helium, and, of course, carbon dioxide that humans continue to combard the atmosphere with as part of pollution.

The air at the Equator rises and expands as it gets its heat from the Sun. Then the air cools down as it blows away from the Equator toward the North and South poles. Some of it, however, returns to the Equator as *trade winds.* Some of it continues moving towards the poles.

On the other hand, the so-called *local winds* cause the changes of weather as a result of heating and cooling the Earth's surface in a particular area. The fact is, warm air rises and cool air moves down, causing air to blow. As already mentioned, such moving air is called the *wind.* You can't see the wind; it just exclaims, "Here I come!"

Products of Changing Weather. Changing weather causes many things—storms, floods, tornadoes, and hurricanes.

A storm is caused by fast-moving hot air that is allergic to any icy cold air it meets. This colliding of the incompatible winds may turn into something else, like a rainstorm, a snowstorm, a monsoon, a thunderstorm, a hurricane, or a tornado.

Descriptions of some of the products of changing weather are as follows:

1. **Thunderstorm.** A *thunderstorm* is a storm accompanied by thunder and lightning. In such a storm, differences in electrical charges build up in clouds as a result of friction. Lightning occurs when the electricity discharges. When this lightning flash strikes the air, it expands and causes a large and loud sound, called *thunder.* In some instances, hailstones, frozen raindrops in the clouds, may fall onto the ground when they are heavy enough.

2. **Hurricane.** A *hurricane* may be described as a violent, tropical cyclone with winds moving at 73 or more miles per hour. Usually, it is accompanied by torrential rains. A hurricane is called a *typhoon* in the Orient.

3. **Tornado.** A *tornado* is a violent, swirling column of air extending downward from the clouds. It uproots trees and blows cars, people, houses, and everything in its path into the air, leaving in its wake death and destruction.

4. **Blizzard.** A *blizzard* is a severe storm involving cold temperatures and heavy, drifting snow.

Volcanoes and Earthquakes

Volcanoes. Deep inside the Earth's mantle, hot molten rocks form magma. When too much magma accumulates, hot gases shoot the magma upward, and it escapes through the Earth's weak crust through holes known as *vents*. The volcanoes spew out the magma for a few days or weeks. When the magma is outside the volcano, it is called *lava*. The red, hot lava then flows downward, covering land, trees, houses, and everything in its path. When it cools down, it becomes hard.

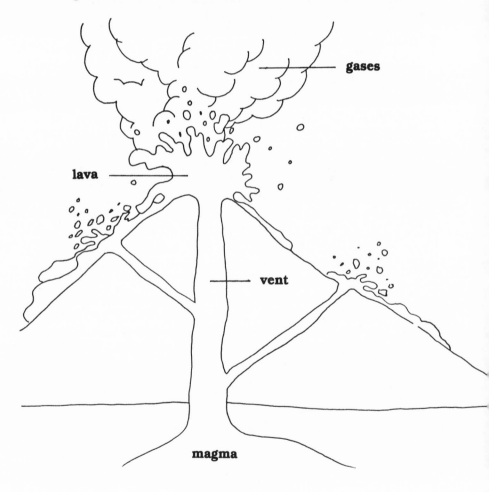

An Erupting Volcano

Earthquakes. "I thought it was the end of the world!" many people say after they have experienced a strong earthquake. Caused by volcanic forces or by the breaking or shifting of rocks under the Earth, an earthquake is the shaking or the trembling of the Earth's surface. This occurs when underground rocks are squeezed by forces caused by the great heat inside. This results in movements along cracks in the rock called *faults*, as if saying, "Move over! Move over!" The rocks in these faults, such as the San Andreas Fault in California, move sideways or upward and downward. When the strain is too much, the rocks break or shift. This causes the trembling of the surface of the Earth.

Classification of Rocks

A *rock* is any accumulation of two or more minerals, consisting of the basic makeup of the Earth. Rocks are solid clusters of minerals (chemical substances composed of crystals). They are divided into three kinds: *sedimentary, igneous,* and *metamorphic.*

1. **Sedimentary Rocks.** *Sedimentary rocks* are formed by the accumulation of mud, sand, and plant and animal remains. As years pass, the mixture gradually hardens into rock as it is buried beneath more and more layers of sediments. An example of a sedimentary rock in seaside cliffs is chalk, a white limestone formed millions of years ago from animal skeletons, including birds, reptiles, and fish. Chalk is also formed from white mud deposits in sea bottoms.

2. **Igneous Rocks.** *Igneous rocks* are formed by the cooling and solidification of molten material from erupted volcanoes.

3. **Metamorphic Rocks.** *Metamorphic rocks* are formed when igneous or sedimentary rocks become hard due to heat, pressure, or chemical changes. An example of metamorphic rock is marble, made of limestone pressed and heated deep inside the Earth.

How Do Rocks Become Soil?

You have seen different kinds of rocks and soils. Maybe you've been wondering how rocks can become soil. Rocks decay and become fine materials of the Earth's surface through the process known as *weathering.* In general terms, weathering is the process by which rocks split up, break into small pieces, and become clay or soil by the interchanging of hot and cold temperatures, water freezing and thawing, and other means.

According to geologists, there are two kinds of weathering.

1. **Physical Weathering.** This is the process by which rocks rot, become fine particles, and combine with other soil by physical means. In some cold areas of the world, there are times that water freezes due to cold weather after a rain. That happens when water seeps into rock cracks, causing the water to freeze and expand, resulting in the breaking of the rock. In hot deserts during the day when the Earth's temperature becomes hot, the rocks become hot, too, causing them to expand. When night falls, cold temperatures replace hot temperatures, causing the rocks to shrink abruptly. Then the rocks break.

2. **Chemical Weathering.** This is the process by which rocks rot through chemical changes caused by water and air. Some gases, such as oxygen and carbon dioxide, may be carried by rain from the atmosphere when it falls. The carbon dioxide causes the rain to be acidic. Such acid dissolves some rocks, like limestone.

The Effects of Erosion

The Earth contains different kinds of soil that cover mountains, hills, grasslands, and lowlands. Made of different minerals, rock particles, and small pieces of decayed plants and animals, the soil is thin and loose. *When it rains, it pours.* The water washes away the mineral-rich topsoil where plants grow. On the other hand, the wind blows away thin soil, leaving rocks. This process is known as *erosion.*

Plant roots hold soil, but most of the trees and other plants in our forests have been cut down, causing the soil to be eroded by water and wind. So the soil is blown away by the wind and washed into brooks, rivers, and seas. Such erosion causes floods, too. So, as you know, people are urged to protect our forests and to plant more trees.

Minerals

Some minerals are solid materials made up of the same chemical substances having distinguished physical properties. They are called *gems* and are made into jewelry and ornaments. An example of a gem is a birthstone, a symbol of the month of a person's birth.

Coal, Oil, and Gas

Millions of years ago, plants were the first inhabitants of the Earth. They were large and abundant in swamps and forests. Then the seas rose, covering the plants in many parts of what was once land. On land, remains of dead plants and animals were also buried by layers and layers of sediments. Such remains were pressed together. Through natural chemical processes, they became oil, coal, and gas. Then man learned how to mine them and to use them for energy.

But deposits of oil, coal, and gas will be soon depleted. Yes, the time is coming when there will be no more oil deposits. Then, there probably won't be any wars in the Middle East over oil and no more Saddam Husseins. The time is coming when humans will turn to the full use of other forms of energy, such as solar and nuclear powers.

Save the Earth!

The Earth is in danger! Cars, trucks, houses, and power plants are burning fuels that emit huge amounts of carbon dioxide into the atmosphere. As already mentioned, there is already too much carbon dioxide in the air, and even more is being accumulated. There are not enough plants on Earth to pump them to use in their photosynthesis for the production of their food. (The plants produce oxygen, the air we breathe.) Thus, the thick layer of carbon dioxide in the atmosphere prevents escaping of the unabsorbed heat above the surface of the Earth into outer space. The Sun continues to shine, and more heat comes to Earth. That's why there is now the so-called warming of the Earth.

Due to this pollution of the air, we are now witnessing some changes in the weather. Scientists are expecting more changes to come. As some scientists say, "Save the Earth!"

What happens next depends on what humans do now and in the years to come!

Physical Science   **17**

Physical science is one of the three branches of science; the other two are life science (living things) and Earth science (Earth and space). In this chapter, we'll discuss elements, matter, energy, motion, heat, light, and sound.

But before we discuss these subjects, here is a list of subject areas taught in physical science in the majority of elementary schools.

Subject Areas

★ ★ ★ ★ ★

Kindergarten

In kindergarten, the classification of objects (matter) by their properties is studied. Also studied are heat, energy, light, and sound.

★ ★ ★ ★ ★

Grade 1

At this grade level, your child should also know how to use color, shape, and size in describing and comparing things. He should also be able to classify items from light to dark or from hot to cold. Also, he should be able to identify sounds in nature and know how to make sounds and listen to sounds.

★ ★ ★ ★ ★

Grade 2

The properties and states of matter should be known by your child at this grade level. Also, he should study well the definition of heat and light energy, the difference between sound and noise, and the movement of sound through air, water, or solids. The study of magnets is a must.

★ ★ ★ ★ ★

Grade 3

By this time, he should be able to discuss all the properties, states, changes, and measurement of matter. The study of work, force, and energy is emphasized at this grade level. The study of heat, light, and sound is continued at this grade level.

★ ★ ★ ★ ★

Grade 4

The study of energy and simple machines is continued at this grade level; such energy includes heat energy. Magnetism is also an important subject area in grade 4.

★ ★ ★ ★ ★

Grade 5

At this grade level, the building blocks of matters—atoms, elements, molecules, and compounds—are fully taught in school. Also, the physical changes in matter is an important part of the topics discussed in the classroom. Also taught in school at this grade level is the understanding of electricity and other sources of energy.

★ ★ ★ ★ ★

Grade 6

The study of matter and atoms—including mass, weight, elements, compounds, acids, and bases—is emphasized in grade 6. The topics studied also include chemical changes in matter, light energy, sound energy, and electricity.

I. Elements

An *element* is a substance composed of only one kind of atom. Elements are divided into two main groups: *metals* and *nonmetals*. As of now, there are 107 known elements. Because metals (aluminum, lead, nickel) have shiny surfaces, they conduct electricity and heat very well. On the other hand, nonmetals (wood, rubber, oxygen, hydrogen) are not shiny, and they don't conduct electricity or heat very well. All atoms in an element have the same atomic number; it is not possible to break up an element into different parts if they have different chemical properties.

An atomic number is the number of protons in a nucleus of an atom. Atoms contain the same number of protons and electrons. For instance, hydrogen has one proton and one electron. In a periodic table made by Russian chemist Dmitri Mendeleev (1834-1907), he classified the elements by their atomic numbers.

The number of atoms (atomic number) in each molecule is represented by a number after the element. For example, the substance of carbon dioxide has one atom of carbon and two atoms of oxygen (CO_2) in each molecule. So all in all, three atoms of two elements make up each molecule of carbon dioxide.

To understand protons and electrons, we must first know the definitions of molecules and atoms.

1. **Molecules.** Molecules are tiny parts of all substances, and they are seen only through powerful microscopes. For instance, a drop of water is made up of billions of molecules. Each of the water molecules is alike. However, molecules of one substance are different from molecules of another substance.

2. **Atoms.** Atoms are small particles that make up molecules. In other words, atoms are smaller than molecules. In the majority of cases, one molecule is made up of several atoms.

For example, one water molecule is made up of two hydrogen atoms and one oxygen atom (H_2O). In the formula, you can see the 2 after the H, meaning that there are two hydrogen atoms and no number after O (oxygen), meaning that there is only one atom. So in the case of water, each molecule is made up of two atoms of hydrogen and one atom of oxygen.

This combination of symbols (H-hydrogen, O-oxygen) and small numbers (1, 2, 3, 12) is called a *formula*. In other words, chemists use a chemical symbol for each element and its number of atoms in each molecule. Such symbols are Zn for zinc, Cl for chlorine, Au for gold, and Mg for magnesium.

Protons, Neutrons, and Electrons. Inside an atom are three smaller kinds of particles: *protons, neutrons,* and *electrons.* The protons and neutrons occupy the center of an atom, called the *nucleus.* On the other hand, electrons are outside the nucleus.

The operation of protons, neutrons, and electrons is always compared to the operation of the Solar System. In the Solar System, the Sun is the center or the nucleus, and the planets, including the Earth, orbit around it. In the case of the atom, protons and neutrons are in the center (the nucleus) of the atom. Electrons revolve around protons and neutrons.

Protons have a positive (+) charge, while electrons have a negative (−) charge. They attract each other because they have opposite charges, but their electrical charges are canceled when they combine. Meanwhile, neutrons have no charge.

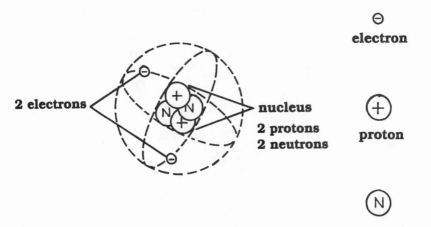

Helium Atom

II. Matter

Matter is anything that has weight and takes up space. Examples of matter are sand and wood. Matter can be weighed, touched, or held.

1. States of Matter

The three states in which matter exists are solid, liquid, and gas. A piece of matter that keeps its shape is called a *solid* (stone, rubber band, pencil), while a piece of matter that has no shape of its own and that flows and pours is called a *liquid* (water, milk, gasoline). On the other hand, *gas* is a matter with no shape at all, but it can be collected in a closed container, or it can roam around in the air (oxygen, carbon dioxide, methane, helium). For example, helium, which like all gases is invisible, is lighter than air. So when it is placed inside a balloon, the balloon rises in the air.

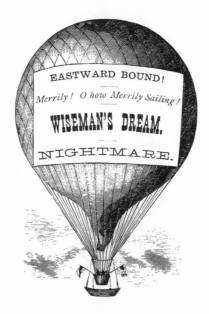

The Balloon Rises in the Air

Properties. Matter has different properties that we use in describing it. Such properties may include size, shape, color, smell, or feel. For example, a ball maybe round or oval, rough or smooth, any color, small or big. Matter can also be bent, cut, broken, or bounced.

2. Chemical Reactions

a. **Compound.** All but six elements combine with other elements to form compounds. A *compound* is a substance of two or more elements. In this combination, each element loses its own special physical and chemical properties and a new compound is formed. The new compound has its own properties.

For example, by themselves, sodium (Na) and chlorine (Cl) are poisonous. However, when you combine them chemically, they form the compound sodium chloride (NaCl), which is called *table salt.*

b. **Mixture.** A *mixture* is the combination of two or more elements or substances, in which each element or compound doesn't lose its own physical or chemical properties. For example, you can combine water with oil, but the mixtures does not change its properties—water is still water, and oil is still oil.

c. **Solution.** A *solution* is any mixture of two substances in which the molecules of one substance are distributed evenly and equally between the molecules of another substance. For instance, when you mix sugar with water, the sugar's molecules spread out equally. Then they move between the water's molecules as if saying, "Give us space! Give us space!" When the water is tasted, it tastes sugar. In other words, sugar dissolves in water. A substance that dissolves is known as a *salute;* the substance that dissolves it is known as a *solvent.*

d. **Change of State.** Many substances change their state when heated or cooled. For instance, water, which is a liquid, can be changed to gas (water vapor) at normal temperatures and can be transformed into a solid (ice) when it is cooled at freezing point.

e. **Combustion.** *Combustion* is a chemical reaction between a gas and another substance. For example, when iron is combined with oxygen in the air, it rusts (like parts of a car); this is called *slow oxidation.* Oxidation can also be accomplished by burning, which produces both light and heat. However, a gas needs another gas to keep burning. For instance, when you light a candle, the paraffin wax produces a vapor (gas) which needs oxygen to keep burning. However, if you cover the candle with a metal or glass jar, the flame vanishes. The reason is, the air inside the jar is exhausted.

3. Acids, Bases, and Salts

a. **Acids.** An *acid* is a chemical compound that has hydrogen and at least one other element. Normally, acids are liquid. For instance, sulfuric acid is made up of hydrogen (H), sulfur (S), and oxygen (O). Its formula is H_2SO_4. That means it has two atoms of hydrogen in each molecule, one atom of sulfur, and four atoms of oxygen. Sulfuric acid is the most useful acid.

However, some acids are so strong that they not only burn skin but also dissolve metals.

b. **Bases.** A *base* is a substance that forms salt-plus-water in reaction with an acid. Generally, most bases are the products of reactions with oxygen and hydrogen, popularly known as *oxides* or *hydroxides* of metals. This is the most known chemical rule about acids and bases:

Acid + Base = Salt + Water

In this case, the acid and the base neutralize each other.

c. **Salts.** When you combine hydrochloric acid (HCl) with sodium hydroxide (NaOH), a base, they become the common form of salt (sodium chloride) and water. In other words, the acid and the base neutralize each other. The formula is this:

Acid		Base		Salt		Water
HCl	+	NaOH	=	NaCl	+	H2O

4. Metals

A *metal* is an element found in the Earth which can be made to shine or have a luster for decoration purposes and other uses. When shined, they conduct heat and electricity easily. About 70 of the known elements are metals.

However, only a few metals can be found in their pure form— gold, platinum, and some copper and silver. The other metals are mined as raw substances known as *ores*. They contain other materials such as oxygen, sulfur, and carbon. Therefore, the pure metal is obtained when the other substances are removed by heating or by electrolysis.

5. Gases

The air is mostly comprised of nitrogen (78 percent), oxygen (about 21 percent), carbon dioxide, water vapor, helium, and other gases. Like carbon dioxide, oxygen dissolves in water. That's why fish can inhale oxygen in the water, whether in rivers or in oceans.

Oxygen. *Oxygen*, which comprises about one-fifth of the atmosphere, is a colorless, odorless gas. That's the gas we inhale. It's produced by plants through photosynthesis—the production of food in their leaves. (See *Photosynthesis* on page 170.)

Carbon Dioxide. *Carbon dioxide* is the gas we exhale and the gas that plants need. It also makes bubbles in drink, such as carbonated drinks.

Methane. *Methane* is a compound of carbon and hydrogen, which is chemically the same as natural gas. We use this for heating our home and for cooking.

Of course, we use other gases, like helium to cause balloons to rise, etc., for other purposes in our daily living.

★ ★ ★ ★ ★

III. Energy and Motion

Energy is the ability to do work or what it takes to get things done. Most of our energy comes from the Sun; it gives us heat and light. This light energy also helps plants to process their food through photosynthesis.

1. Energy from Food

As mentioned above, plants process their food through photosynthesis in their leaves. Animals, on the other hand, take in food, cooked or uncooked (like hamburger or salad), into the stomach. When digested, the dissolved food is distributed by blood throughout the body for its nourishment, thus giving energy we need to walk, run, play, or work.

2. Energy from Simple Machines

A *machine* is a device we use to help us do our work. The five simple machines are the *lever*, the *wedge*, the *wheel* and *axle*, *the pulley*, the *screw* and the *gear*. The first two were used even by people of the Stone Age 100,000 years ago. Wood rollers were used as wheels by the Egyptians to move huge stones in building their pyramids. But the actual wheel we know today was discovered later; it became popular only about 5,000 years ago.

1. **Lever.** A *lever* is a pole or a bar which is used to lift or to pry in order to move something from one place to another. A lever works this way: The object to be moved is called the *load*, and the force needed to move it is called the *effort*. But this can't be done without the pivot or the fulcrum. The simplest lever, used even by people of long ago, was a branch of a tree resting on a small rock (the fulcrum) to lift a much heavier object. The lever is also used when you use simple levers such as a pair of scissors to cut something or use a piece of wood or metal to open a paint can. Of course, there are other simple or improved levers whose principle of operation is the same.

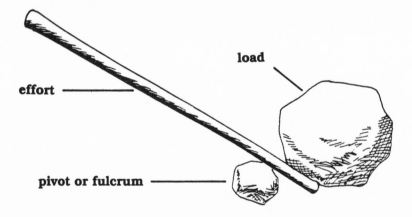

The Lever

2. **Wedge.** A *wedge* is a piece of hard material, metal or wood, used to split wood, lift a weight, or reinforce a structure. Stone Age people used wedges to split wood. (Many people today still use wedges to split wood.) They also used the wedge to split soil for farming. Other forms of wedges are ax blades, chisels, and knives. A scythe, for instance, is both a lever and a wedge, the handle being the lever and the blade the wedge.

The Wedge

3. **Wheel and Axle.** Of course, a wheel is round; it turns around a rod known as an *axle* that moves through its center. Even during ancient times, the Egyptians used wooden rollers (the equivalent of wheels) to push heavy loads of stone while building their pyramids. Some examples of wheels are those used to move wheelbarrows, carts, cars, trucks, and trains. They are all around us.

The Wheel and Axle

4. **Pulley.** A *pulley* is a wheel that is turned by a belt, a rope, a chain, etc., to change the direction of force. For instance, you can lift a load upward with much easier effort by having a rope running over a pulley wheel and then pulling the rope downward. With a combination of wheels and with only one continuous rope or chain running through them, you can lift a greater load with the same effort.

5. **Screw.** A *screw* is any one of various devices operating or threaded like a simple screw that is spiraled or twisted to move or operate things. If you use a screw jack, you can lift a car easily off the ground. Of course, the jack has a handle that turns the screw. (In this case, the handle also acts as a lever.)

6. **Gear.** A *gear* is a combination of a screw and a wheel. It is a toothed wheel or disk designed to mesh with another so that the motion of one controls the speed and torque of another in order to move things, such as the one shown below.

Force and Motion. If you want to move an object, you need force. For example, you may make a simple pendulum by tying a small piece of a stone with a piece of string. Holding the end of the string with your right hand, you may push the other end of the string holding the stone with your left hand. Then the force of your push creates motion—swinging the stone up and down. *Inertia* keeps the movement going until the pendulum's motion is stopped by another strong force, which is *gravity*. In other words, all moving objects have their own inertia—they keep moving until another force stops them.

3. Energy from Fuel

Fuel is matter that is burned to produce energy. Of course, the most important fuels are oil, coal, and natural gas. They are the byproducts of plants and animals that were buried millions of years ago.

4. Energy from Wind, Water, Nuclear Power, Magnets, and Electricity

Of course, we also get energy from wind and water. Wind can fly kites, move sailboats, and turn windmills to move water for irrigation purposes.

Water can also produce electricity which, in turn, gives light and runs factories.

For instance, a dam is built across a river with strong currents. A huge volume of water is trapped behind the dam, but a portion of the water is allowed to overflow. The powerful falling water turns wheels that operate *generators*. These change the energy of the falling water into electrical energy. Then the electrical energy passes through wires bound for homes, offices, and factories.

As you can see, electrical energy, through the use of appliances and other equipment, is used for heating, cooling, washing, drying, lighting, toasting, and other things.

Nuclear Power. Nuclear power plants now produce electricity. In the future, solar power will be harnessed to produce energy.

Magnets. A *magnet* is a piece of metal with two poles, north and south, near its end. It is used to attract another substance. Of course, iron and steel make good magnets. Unlike poles (north and south) attract each other, while like poles (north and north, or south and south) repel each other.

An example of a magnet is a compass, which always points toward the magnetic North Pole. The Earth is the largest magnet of all!

Magnetism and Electricity. In many ways, magnetism and electricity are alike. However, a big difference lies in the fact that the force between two magnetic objects is not affected by the material that separates them. On the other hand, the force between two electrically charged objects is affected by whether the separating material is a good or poor conductor of electricity.

For instance, an electric motor turns electrical energy into mechanical energy with the help of a magnet. It works this way: A coil, called an *armature*, is fixed on an axle between the poles of a magnet. When the current starts to pass through the coil, the armature rotates and keeps moving as long as the flow of current isn't stopped.

★ ★ ★ ★ ★

IV. Heat, Light, and Sound

1. Heat

Heat is motion. Like light and sound, heat is a form of energy. Most of the time, it is the twin of light. When the Sun shines brightly, you see the light, but you only feel the heat.

As mentioned in the early part of this chapter, molecules are always moving. When a quarterback is cold during a football game, he rubs his left hand with his right hand, and the moving molecules in his left hand are speeded up by the molecules in his right hand. Thus, the energy that moves from his right hand to his left hand causes the heat. He feels the heat. In other words, rubbing things together produces heat or even fire in the case of two pieces of wood.

Heat can also expand or take up more space. For instance, when you heat the air inside a hot-air balloon, the hot, moving molecules cause the balloon to expand and rise into the air.

A heater in your house brings hot air into your rooms. The warm air moves away from the heater and rises. Then the air cools and it begins to fall to the floor and then causes the warm air from the heater to move, thus circulating the new warm air inside the house. That's how heat is circulated.

Of course, you use heat all the time: cooking meals, drying clothes, etc.

2. Light

Light is an electromagnetic radiation that can be seen by the human eye. Like heat, it is a form of energy. Light energy comes from the Sun, heaters, fires, light bulbs, and many other things. It moves in waves through the air or outer space.

You can see light through your eyes. Light enters through the pupils, the black dots in the center of the eyes. Then the light is transmitted through nerve cells to the brain. Then the brain tells you what you see. "There's Omar Khadafy on the TV screen!" your brain might say.

Bending of Light. Light is bent when it is reflected or bounced back from a surface, such as a mirror. This bending is called *reflection*.

For instance, when the Sun hits the Moon, the light is bounced or reflected to the Earth. On the other hand, when light is bent while traveling from one transparent surface to another, it is called *refraction*.

One example of light being bent is the work done by magnifying glasses and telescopes that have lenses that bend light. As a result, they make things smaller or bigger.

Prisms can bend light in another way: They bend white light into colors of the rainbow.

3. Sound

Like heat and light, *sound* is a form of energy. It travels in waves like light. However, it needs something to travel through, like air or any substance with molecules that move. Therefore, unlike light, sound cannot travel in a vacuum like outer space. Sound cannot travel on the surface of the Moon because the Moon has no air.

When things vibrate or move back and forth, their molecules collide with all the molecules around them, moving them in all directions. That's how sound travels. In a nutshell, sound travels through third parties, like air, wood, water—anything with moving molecules in them.

Of course, there are high and low sounds. When you whisper sweet nothings into the ear of your loved one, that's only a low sound. The sound of a jet plane during its liftoff is very loud. The loudness or lowness of sound is called *pitch*. Scientists measure the loudness of sound in decibels; sounds louder than 85 decibels can hurt a human's ears.

Things and animals produce sounds. However, they make their own sounds in different ways. For instance, the sound emanating from a guitar is different from the sound from a flute. Or the sound made by a bird is different from the sound produced by a dog.

Sound travels slower than light. For instance, when you see the explosion of something several miles away, you see the flash of light before your ears hear the sound. The speed of sound is about 1,100 feet per second.

Like light, sound also bounces, which is called an *echo*. For example, when you're inside an old cathedral or a cave and you shout, "Saddam! Saddam!" the sound you produce may bounce back to you. That is an echo. It is caused by sound waves bouncing off the hard walls of the cathedral or the cave and entering your ears.

Conclusion

As you can see, the study of physical science is important to your child. His thorough knowledge of this science will make him aware of the importance of energy and other resources of the earth in daily living.

If you teach him very well, he'll not only get A's in science, but he'll also know how to properly use energy and other resources and how to conserve them for the benefit of generations to come.

Unit V—Social Studies

Introduction to
  Social Studies
Geography
History
Government

Introduction to Social Studies   18

The major subject areas involving social studies are geography, history, and government. In some schools, economics, sociology, and psychology are also included in social studies.

In general, the major subject areas in social studies at different grade levels are as follows: kindergarten—himself/herself; grade 1—family and friends; grade 2—neighborhood; grade 3—city, town, and state; grade 4—regions of the country and the world; grade 5—the country's history; and grade 6—the world, eastern hemisphere, and western hemisphere.

For the purpose of studying social studies, we shall discuss the above subject matters in the following three chapters.

Geography

Your child should know the topography of the Earth in order to know how we use its resources. He needs to understand and learn basic geographic facts and concepts to know how he and his fellow human beings can react to them.

History

History is the study of the past.   In simple words, one may not know where he's going if he doesn't know where he came from. Knowing one's history, a student will know the traditions and heritage of his own race or ethnic group, and he can learn from the lessons of the past in order to shape his dream of the future.

Government

The study of government is a must for your child so that he can learn our system of government and how it works. He needs to know that in order to live in a democratic country, in particular, and in a society, as a whole, there must be some kind of order and organization of its citizenry.

★ ★ ★ ★ ★

Subject Areas

Kindergarten

Geography

In kindergarten, your child needs to know some aspects of the environment—landforms, bodies of water, weather, climate, and seasons (summer, winter, spring, and fall). He should know how to follow directions (such as east, west, south, or north) and location words (such as over-under and inside-outside). Learning various kinds of transportation is also a must.

History

Holidays and different histories are discussed.

Government

It is emphasized in kindergarten that people live in a society. They live and work together, cooperating with each other to get things done well in the home, in the school, in the community, and at work.

★ ★ ★ ★ ★

Grade 1

Geography

At this grade level, your child needs to understand that maps and globes represent actual places and things (such as mountains, hills, plains, oceans, and rivers). He should also understand simple directions (such as south, north, west, and east) and location words (such as top-bottom).

He should also understand the concepts of day and night and the four seasons—summer, winter, spring, and fall—and what causes them.

History

In this grade, your child should know why we celebrate holidays and why museums are where artifacts or information of the past is deposited.

Government

He should learn by this time that families and schools promulgate rules and that such rules should be obeyed. Also, he needs to learn that people live in communities, and they must know how to work together for the benefit of the majority.

★ ★ ★ ★ ★

Grade 2

Geography

By this time, your child should be familiar with regional differences in climates and why land areas are divided into towns, cities, states, or countries. He should also learn map keys (such as colors, lines, symbols, and points) and how to use simple bar graphs and pictographs.

History

He should learn that our neighborhoods today are different from the neighborhoods of yesteryear. Also, he should know that all Americans, except native Indians, migrated to this country from countries abroad.

Government

He should learn why we hold elections and why a group of officials should rule a town, a city, a state, or a country.

★ ★ ★ ★ ★

Grade 3

Geography

In studying climate, topography, and natural resources of a certain region or state, your child should know the different kinds of maps—road, climate, product, weather, etc. By this time, he should also know how to locate the Equator and the Northern and Southern hemispheres.

He should learn how to collect original data to make a simple graph, chart, or diagram.

History

He should know why our life today is different from the life of yesterday due to technology.

Government

He should learn why a good government can make a cummunity or region progressive.

★ ★ ★ ★ ★

Grade 4

Geography

At this grade level, your child should know the various types of topography, climate, and natural resources of the United States and the world.

History

He should learn that each region of the United States has a colorful history.

Government

He should learn that although the American people came from different countries with different cultural backgrounds, they can live and work together as one people in one country.

★ ★ ★ ★ ★

Grade 5

Geography

In this grade, your child should know how different aspects of topography have influenced how people live in particular regions of the country, thus resulting in some differences.

History

He needs to learn the history of the United States, which will lead to his understanding of how this country was explored, populated, and industrialized, resulting in its becoming a world power. Learning the history of other nations in North America and South America is also a must.

Government

He should know that democracy is still the best form of government in the world. Teach him that it was this principle that caused the British and other nationalities to come and live free in this country.

★ ★ ★ ★ ★

Grade 6

Geography

At this grade level, your child should know why and how climate and/or landforms influence the lifestyles of people living in certain localities or regions. He also needs to learn how or why people live in a particular region.

History

He should learn that every nation is making a contribution to the betterment of the world.

Government

He should know that although different countries have different political ideologies, they all have laws promulgated by the authorities under their own kind of government.

Geography **19**

Geography is the science that deals with the surface of the Earth and its divisions into continents and countries. It covers Earth's natural resources, plants, animals, inhabitants, weather, and industries.

This is an important part of social studies in the sense that human activity is affected by the environment's physical features in a particular area. Your child must know basic geographic facts and concepts to understand the Earth and its environment and how to interact with them. For instance, landforms, such as mountains, hills, and plains, affect his movement; some of them may be a hindrance to his travel. Knowing his own region's environment, he'll have the ability to make use of its resources and interact with people around him or in his state, region, or country.

Generally speaking, your child, in studying geography, will learn how to locate physical and cultural patterns on the Earth's surface. He'll also learn the patterns of population and migration.

See chapter 18 for subject areas covered in different grades.)

★ ★ ★ ★ ★

I. Maps and Globes

The main directions, known as *cardinal directions*, are north, south, east, and west. The directions between the four cardinal directions are known as *intermediate directions*. They are northeast or NE, which is between north and east; northwest or NW, which is between north and west; southeast or SE, which is between south and east; and southwest or SW, which is between south and west.

Map

A *map* is a picture drawn on a flat surface which shows places and things—how they look and where they are. In other words, it represents places and things in miniature form. For instance, when you draw the inside of your room showing furniture and other things, you're making a map. Also, you can make a community map that shows the important roads or buildings in your locality. And there are city, state, country, and world maps. There are also other kinds of maps, such as physical, political, product, weather, road, and time zone.

1. **Physical Map.** A *physical map* shows landforms, including mountains, hills, plains, plateaus, and other features of the Earth's surface. It includes water forms, such as oceans, rivers, lakes, and harbors. It also shows the elevation (or height) of the land in relation to the level of the sea (called *sea level).* In some physical maps, patterns or colors are indicated. For instance, *isolines* are lines that indicate equal distances or elevations in certain places—particularly in hilly or mountainous areas. However, they are called *contour lines* when the isolines indicate elevations on a contour map.

2. **Political Map.** A *political map* of the United States shows the different states and indicates the boundaries between them.

3. **Product Map.** A *product map* shows different products, produced on land and from underground, such as minerals, with symbols to represent what they are.

4. **Weather Map.** A *weather map* shows the different temperatures (whether hot, cold, or warm) in different places indicated in the map key.

5. **Road Map.** A *road map* shows freeways, highways, streets, railroads, and important landmarks to show locations in a town, a city, a county, or a country.

6. **Time Zone Map.** A *time zone map* shows the different times of the day or the night in different states or countries. Excluding Alaska and Hawaii, which have their own time zones, there are four time zones in the continental United States—Pacific Time, Mountain Time, Central Time, and Eastern Time. There is an hour difference from zone to zone; for instance, when it's three o'clock in Nevada (Pacific Time), it's

four o'clock in Wyoming (Mountain Time), five o'clock in Iowa
(Central Time), and six o'clock in Ohio (Eastern Time).

A Time Zone Map

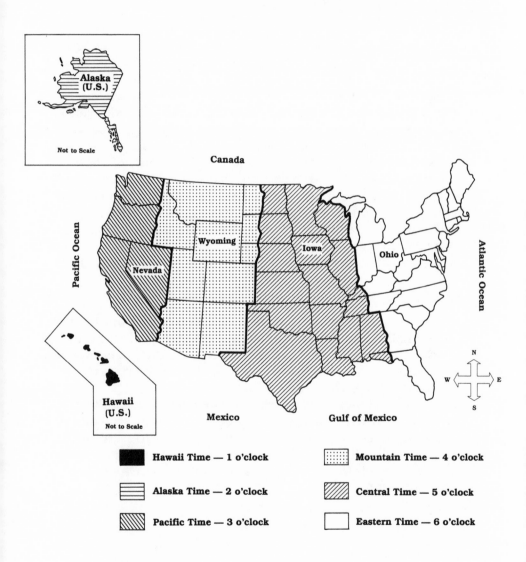

Featured in every map are the following:

a. *Compass Rose.* The *compass rose* is a direction finder which is included in a map. It is a drawing showing four arrows with the words North, South, West, and East, or N, S, W, and E. Without it, you won't know which is N, S, W, or E.

b. *Map Key.* The map key shows symbols representing places or things, such as rivers, railroads, buildings, and roads.

c. *Map Scale.* Most maps are drawn to scale. That is, map makers draw maps showing distances between places. For instance, in a certain map, an inch may represent ten miles, which is the actual distance. With this kind of guide, you'll know the actual distance if you measure it in a straight line with a ruler. Of course, if you actually go there by car, the actual distance is longer because of winding roads. But, of course, there are maps which indicate the actual road distance, too.

d. *Grid.* Sometimes a map has vertical and horizontal lines which form connected squares or blocks. These lines form a grid which represents blocks of space. You can use letters and numbers on a grid to name the blocks or the squares, such as ABC downward (vertical) and 123 going across (horizontal).

Globe

A *globe* is a round ball that shows the whole world around it, including land and water. A different kind of map, it's a picture of the Earth, tilted on a stand. When you turn the globe, which is mounted to the stand, it shows how the Earth orbits on its axis as it rotates around the Sun.

The globe shows different parts of the Earth. You can see all the seven continents on a globe. In one part, you can see—at the same time—four continents, Europe, Asia, Africa, and Australia, as well as a part of Antarctica. In one part, you can see the two continents, North America and South America, and the other part of Antarctica.

North America

Arctic Ocean

Greenland

Alaska (U.S.)

Pacific Ocean

Canada

Atlantic Ocean

United States

N
W — E
S

Mexico

1. **Equator.** The *Equator* is the imaginary line between the North Pole (top) and the South Pole (bottom) that divides the Earth. Everything above the Equator (north) is called the *Northern Hemisphere;* everything below the Equator (south) is called the *Southern Hemisphere.*

2. **Meridians or Longitudes.** These are imaginary lines from the North Pole to the South Pole that run halfway around the Earth. The *Prime Meridian* or *first meridian* and the *180th meridian* are on opposite sides of the Earth. They divide our planet into the *Eastern Hemisphere* and the *Western Hemisphere.* Meridians that go to the left and right of the Prime Meridian are labeled with numbers from 0 degrees, starting at the Prime Meridian, up to 180 degrees on the opposite side of

the planet. The Prime Meridian passes through the countries of England, Spain, and Ghana. It is also known as the Greenwich Meridian because it cuts through Greenwich, England.

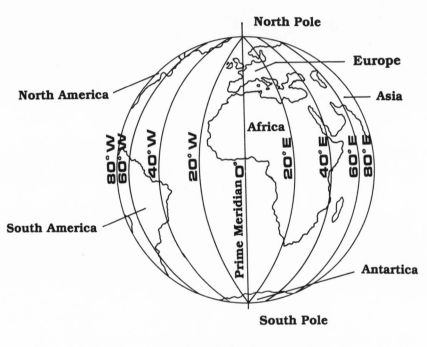

Meridians or Longitudes

3. **Parallels or Lines of Latitude.** These are imaginary lines from east to west (not north to south as in the case of meridians) that encircle the Earth. The main line of latitude with the 0 degree that divides the Earth is the Equator. All other lines are parallel to the Equator. Like the meridians, parallels are identified by numbers and the degree symbol.

It is through the above longitudes and latitudes that locations are pinpointed on land and at sea. It was through this means that Allied troops, who were not familiar with the Arabian Desert, were able to know their routes to attack the Iraqis.

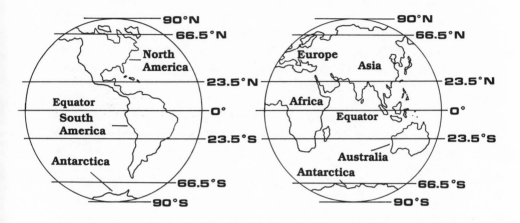

Parallels or Lines of Latitude

II. Land Forms

Water covers about 70 percent of the Earth's surface, surrounding seven large bodies of land, which we call continents. These continents are Africa, Europe, Asia, Australia, Antarctica, South America, and North America. They are actually the tops of huge plates of land and rocks covered by oceans. On the other hand, the surface land features are called landforms. The major landforms are mountains, hills, plateaus, and plains.

1. **Mountains.** With raised and sloping sides and usually with forests, they average over 2,000 feet in elevation.

2. **Hills.** Also with raised and sloping sides, hills average under 2,000 feet.

3. **Plateaus.** With flat or rolling land, plateaus average over 2,000 feet in height.

4. **Plains.** With flat or rolling land, plains average under 2,000 feet in elevation and are usually farmlands.

III. Land Regions of the World

As already mentioned, the seven continents are Africa, Antarctica, Asia, Australia, Europe, North America, and South America. They are also called the different land regions of the world. The biggest region is Asia, which comprises about 30 percent of the world's land area. North America, where the United States is located, has about 15 percent of the total world's land area.

North America and South America occupy almost half of the world. However, most of their areas are covered by water, the Pacific Ocean and the Atlantic Ocean. On the other half of the world are the other five continents.

To the south of the United States is Mexico; to its north is Canada. Near the North Pole is Greenland. On the other hand, South America contains the so-called Latin American countries.

★ ★ ★ ★ ★

IV. Regions of the United States

Geographical Regions

The *geographical regions* of the United States are the Pacific Coast states, the Rocky Mountain states, the Southwestern states, the Midwestern states, the Southern states, the Middle Atlantic states, and the New England states. Alaska and Hawaii, not part of the mainland, may be included in the Pacific states or separately.

The seven geographical regions of states are based on their proximity to each other and their physical features. For instance, the Rocky Mountain states are those in a western mountainous region.

1. **Pacific Coast States.** Including California, Oregon, and Washington, the Pacific Coast states occupy the Pacific mountain ranges and lowlands and cover the far western part of the United States. To their west is the Pacific Ocean. Oregon and Washington also occupy parts of the so-called western plateaus, basins, and ranges.

2. **Rocky Mountain States.** The Rocky Mountain states are Montana, Idaho, Wyoming, Nevada, Utah, and Colorado.

3. **Southwestern States.** The Southwestern states include Arizona, New Mexico, Oklahoma, and Texas.

4. **Midwestern States.** The Midwestern states comprise the "Great Plains," including forests and fertile farmland. These states are North Dakota, South Dakota, Nebraska, Kansas, Minnesota, Iowa, Missouri, Wisconsin, Illinois, Michigan, Indiana, and Ohio.

5. **Southern States.** Known as "The South," this region includes Arkansas, Louisiana, Kentucky, Tennessee, Mississippi, Alabama, Virginia, West Virginia, North Carolina, South Carolina, Georgia, and Florida.

6. **Middle Atlantic States.** The Middle Atlantic states include New York, Pennsylvania, New Jersey, Maryland, and Delaware.

7. **New England States.** The New England states include Vermont, New Hampshire, Maine, Massachusetts, Rhode Island, and Connecticut.

The Middle Atlantic and New England states are sometimes called the Northeastern states.

Political Regions of the United States

The United States is divided into *political regions,* with the major regions being the Pacific, the Northwest, the Southwest, the North Central, the South Central, the Northeast (including New England), and the Southeast. Usually, these regional divisions are used by government offices, such as the U.S. Postal Service.

Geographical Regions of the United States

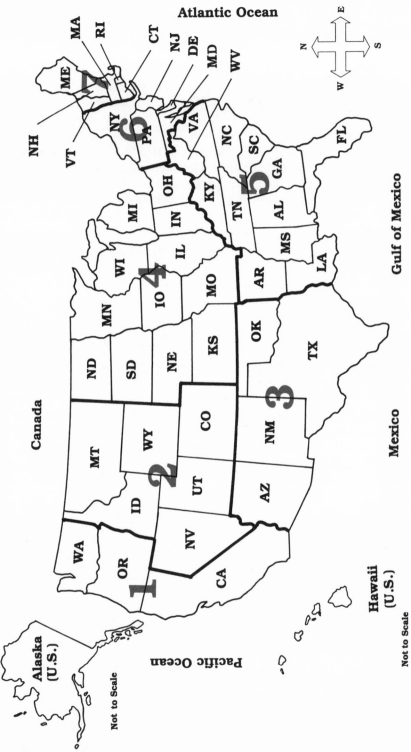

V. Neighborhoods

Of course, regions start as neighborhoods; neighborhoods become towns or cities; then cities to counties; counties to states; and states to countries.

The Invisible Boundaries

In a map, we have boundaries. A *boundary* is usually an imaginary line dividing lands between neighbors, towns, cities, states, or countries. Boundaries between countries are called *international boundaries.* A boundary is usually represented by dotted or plain lines on the map.

Of course, you share boundaries with your neighbors. For example, to the east of your house, you may share a boundary with a neighbor; to the west, with another neighbor; to the south, with another neighbor; and to the north, with a common land—the street, which is a public property.

Sometimes, a boundary is a road or a highway. Other times, boundaries are made by nature; that is why they are called *natural boundaries.* Such boundaries are seas, rivers, lakes, and streams.

Boundaries, although they are only imaginary lines, are important because people, as well as countries, should know what lands, rivers or seas, belong to them. For instance, nations fight for natural resources in certain places or regions. Saddam Hussein of Iraq said, "This land is mine!" But Iran responded, "This land is ours!" and their respective soldiers fought with guns, missiles, and bombs. The war ended after eight years. No one won!

Neighborhoods

States are comprised of many cities, which are comprised of many neighborhoods. A *neighborhood* is a certain place composed of several blocks of houses and buildings where groups of people live. Sometimes, you may greet a neighbor (who lives in a house near yours), "Hi, how are you?" Your neighbor may answer, "Fine, thank you. I think it's a nice day today!" And then you may exchange some words about work, basketball, or whatever. After that brief encounter, you both go to your own homes or places of work.

People who live in a neighborhood share resources with each other. Their children go to the same school; their families go to the same church or the same shopping mall, which you share with some people from other neighborhoods.

There are several—or many—neighborhoods in a town or a city and many neighborhoods in a state. And states make up countries.

Canada, the country to the north of the United States, is composed of provinces, instead of states.

How People Use Land

There are certain factors why people live in a certain state. They probably live there because of the natural resources in that area. Or they like the landforms—lakes, rivers, or plains. Or they like the weather. You, too, right now live in your city or state because you like the landforms, climate, or natural resources—or perhaps because you've always lived there, or your work took you there, or family and friends are there.

People use natural resources directly by farming, lumbering, or fishing. Other times, they manufacture natural resources into finished products. Additionally, people or businesses offer services that make use of natural resources. That's why communities thrive!

Neighboring Countries

Of course, states share resources with neighboring states. Even neighboring countries, too. The United States exports goods to Mexico and Canada, and it imports some goods from them, too. Not only that, different nations import and export goods. We import oil from several countries, but we also export cars, machinery, and other products to other countries. In a nutshell, we share the wealth of Planet Earth with countries of other continents, too.

Conclusion

Help your child to become well acquainted with geography. Let him know the natural resources of your state so that he'll know how to make use of them. Furthermore, he should be familiar with the people, the landforms, the capital cities, and the tourist attractions in other states.

History 20

"Without knowing your past, you won't know your future." That's what some people say, which is why we're studying history—the history of the United States in particular.

The history of our country is a long one. But it's full of adventure, drama, and excitement. That's why some stories of our past have been depicted and dramatized on television or large theater screens. One such story was *North and South.*

The Colonizers of North America

In the 1400s, many Europeans knew about Europe, parts of Africa, and a small portion of Asia. Because they wanted to find a new way to Asia, some adventurers, called *explorers,* tried to sail to Asia. Instead, they discovered the New World—North America and South America. Some of those explorers are mentioned below.

1. **Spain**

a. *Christopher Columbus.* Although he was an Italian by birth, through the courtesy of Isabella, the Queen of Spain, Christopher Columbus sailed on August 3, 1492, for an exploration of new lands. His reason for coming here was not ascertained, but some historians say he was seeking a western route to China and India. Instead of asking the question, "Where's the beef?" his favorite question was, "Where are gold, silks, and spices?" When Columbus landed on an island near North America, he named the people already living there "Indians" because he thought he was in India, a part of Asia. Then he sailed as far as the land of Fidel Castro, Cuba, about 90 miles from the coast of Florida. All in all, he made three more voyages to the so-called *New World.*

b. *Ponce de Leon.* Dubbed as the first Spaniard to extensively explore North America, Ponce de Leon came here seeking a place where he would never grow old—the Fountain of

Youth. He discovered Florida in 1513. Upon coming ashore and viewing the land, he might have said, "This land is for Spain!" Thus, Florida became the property of Spain.

2. *France*

a. *Giovanni Verrazano.* By 1524, in the name of France, Giovanni Verrazano, who was actually a native of what was to become Sophia Loren's country, Italy, toured the North American coast of Newfoundland, near Canada.

b. *Jacques Cartier.* Verrazano was followed by Jacques Cartier, who explored the Gulf of St. Lawrence and the St. Lawrence River. Afterwards, France claimed Canada and the area between the Mississippi River and the Appalachian Mountains.

3. *The Netherlands*

Henry Hudson. Henry Hudson, a British national was given money by the Dutch to search for a northwest passage to Asia. He explored parts of the Hudson River in what is now known as the state of New York. Then some Dutch settled on the island of Manhattan and called it *New Amsterdam.* But in 1655, the British said, "Get out!" and New Amsterdam became theirs.

The Days of Exploration

The Thirteen Colonies

The following account does not give the exact order in which the original thirteen English colonies were founded, but it is a general history of their establishment.

By 1620, the English had already settled in New England. These particular settlers were called Puritans because they wanted to "purify" the Church of England that had separated from Rome. Persecuted in Britain because they wanted to separate from the state church, they went to Holland, then to North America. They settled at Cape Cod Bay, which they called Plymouth in honor of Plymouth, England, their homeland. Actually, they landed there by mistake; they were supposed to be brought by their ship, the *Mayflower*, to an already established colony in Virginia, Jamestown. After fighting aboard ship because they got lost, they signed a document consisting of rules for living in a new land. They called the document the *Mayflower Compact*.

They planted crops, and when they had a good harvest, three days were set aside for celebration. We owe to them *Thanksgiving Day* as we know it today, although the very first Thanksgiving was celebrated at Berkeley Plantation on the James River in Virginia several years before the Pilgrims landed at Plymouth.

Then, one by one, New England was settled. Most of the Puritans settled on the land beside Massachusetts Bay. Some of them founded other colonies—Rhode Island, New Hampshire, and Connecticut. Massachusetts at that time included what was later to become the state of Maine.

Several colonies were established in places now known as New York, Pennsylvania, Maryland, and Delaware. New York, New Jersey, and Delaware were taken from the Dutch by the British in 1664. These states are known today as the Middle Atlantic states.

Southern colonies, such as Virginia, North Carolina, South Carolina, and Georgia grew. The soil and weather in the south were good for agriculture, so colonies raised crops of rice, cotton, and tobacco. The land was so large that they needed additional workers, so they bought many Africans from merchants in the West Indies and used them as slaves. Some of the colonists became very wealthy.

(The original 13 colonies were Massachusetts, Rhode Island, New Hampshire, Connecticut, New York, Pennsylvania, Maryland, Delaware, New Jersey, Virginia, North Carolina, South Carolina, and Georgia. For the dates of their establishment as states, see pages 241.)

When the original thirteen English colonies were established, England began imposing taxes on them, with the support of the British Army stationed in North America. Britain also made moves to restrict the movement of people to the West. Moreover, the colonies were not represented in the Parliament in England.

The Boston Tea Party. Samuel Adams and some rebellious American colonists, disguised as Indians, dumped into Boston Harbor a shipment of tea owned by the British East India Company. It was in protest against the Tea Act passed by the British Parliament in April 1773, which imposed a tax on tea. Then, Parliament passed laws that included the shutting off of the city's sea trade pending payment for the destroyed tea.

Nothing could now stop the colonies from their dream to become an independent nation!

"We Should Be Free! We Should Be Free!"

The Revolutionary War

Finally, the war broke out. (The American Revolution lasted from 1775 to 1783). The Continental Army was led by General George Washington. On April 18, 1775, the first battles were fiercely fought at Lexington and Concord, towns on the outskirts of Boston, Massachusetts. In the meantime, George Washington and his army marched to Dorchester Heights near Boston. The British got scared and left the city.

Then other battles took place. One night, Paul Revere rode through the town shouting, "The British are coming! The British are coming!"

"The British Are Coming! The British Are Coming!

The Declaration of Independence. On July 4, 1776, while the Revolutionary War was raging between the colonies and Great Britain, the colonies signed the Declaration of Independence. John Hancock was the first to sign. On the committee that drafted the document were men such as Thomas Jefferson, John Adams, and Benjamin Franklin. Actually, it was Jefferson who first drafted the Declaration of Independence. When he had finished, he showed it to the others.

Later, they made several changes. Specifically, the document was about the forming of a new country, with its own laws and leaders. The colonists sent the document to the King of England. Of course, the war continued.

Then the colonists established two new models of government—a national government and a state government. They renamed the colonies as states and elected state representatives.

THOMAS JEFFERSON.

The Last Battle. On October 19, 1781, the last major battle took place at Yorktown, Virginia. It was in this battle that France sided with the United States and helped to defeat the British army after three weeks of battle in that locality.

The Treaty of Paris was signed in 1783—a treaty that ended Britain's rule of the land south of Canada.

The Confederation. By 1786, the colonies established a new government for all the states and called it a *confederation*. As a whole, the states were called the *United States of America*.

In 1787, representatives from the confederation held a meeting, called the *Constitutional Convention*, in Philadelphia, Pennsylvania. They wrote the Constitution and then they returned to their home states to present it to their people. Later, a Bill of Rights was included in the Constitution.

The New Nation

Three Branches of Government. A new nation, with a new government, was born after the Revolutionary War. George Washington became the first President of the United States. The government was divided into three branches: *Executive* (President), *Legislative* (Congress), and *Judiciary* (Courts). (Under this system of government in a democratic country, which is still in practice today, the President executes the laws of the land, the Congress makes the laws, and the Courts interpret the laws.)

Political Parties. Because different groups of people had their own opinions on how the government should be run, political parties emerged. By 1876, there were two political parties: Federalists and Republicans. The Federalists, some of whom were businessmen, wanted a strong federal government. On the other hand, the Republicans, many of whom were farmers and lived in the South and the West, wanted strong state governments. Later, other minor parties were organized. (Today, there are only two major political parties: Republicans and Democrats.)

The Need for Expansion

"Go West!" was the battle cry. Although there were already thirteen states, the United States owned more land westward to the Mississippi River.

The Louisiana Territory. However, France owned the land west of the Mississippi River, which was known as the Louisiana Territory. The western settlers used the big river to transport their products to the East Coast. But the time came when France closed this river to shipping. Thomas Jefferson, who was then President, had a solution. He bought the so-called Louisiana Territory for $15,000,000. That purchase almost doubled the size of the United States! Then 18 years later, the United States bought Florida from Spain.

The Oregon Trail. Many people started westward, following the Oregon Trail. "On to Oregon!" was the battle cry snowballing around the country. People had heard of the rich land in Oregon and, in 1843, about a thousand pioneers started moving westward. "Oregon, here we come!" they said.

But that time, both the United States and England claimed the territory. However, no war took place between the nations—they compromised. The United States acquired Oregon, and England acquired Canada, which was ruled by Great Britain until its independence.

The Oregon Trail was one of the great emigrant routes to the Northwest, running from Independence, Missouri, to the Columbia River region of Oregon. It was about 2,000 miles of rugged terrain, including desert and Indian territory. It became the route to the West by some 12,000 emigrants to Oregon from the East. The eastern portion of the trail also became the route to California by gold seekers in the late 1840s. Pioneers had found their destiny!

"Oregon, Here We Come!"

The Texas Country. In 1821, Spain ruled Mexico. But in 1822, Mexico (which included Texas) got its independence from Spain. Stephen Austin, with 300 people, went to Texas to establish a colony. Soon other Anglo-Americans, mostly slave-owning Southerners, followed them.

The American population grew. By 1835, Texas already had several towns populated by Mexicans and Americans. The Americans objected to some laws passed by the Mexican Government and later requested the government to make Texas a separate state in Mexico with its own government. In an answer to this, the Mexican Government passed a law that prohibited any more Americans settling in the area. Then the Americans objected.

War broke out when a group of American volunteers attacked the Mexican fort at Gonzales and drove the Mexican army out of town. Afterwards, the Americans rushed to San Antonio and won several battles.

The dictator of Mexico, General Antonio Lopez de Santa Anna, went himself to Texas with an army, arriving there February 23, 1836. They camped around the Spanish mission, the Alamo, where American volunteers sought refuge.

For 11 days, Santa Anna and his men camped around the mission. The Mexicans, numbering about 3,000, swarmed the fort. Many of them might have shouted, "Viva Mexico!" But the Texans in the fort would not surrender. They fought hard and furious. Some of them might have said, "Over our dead bodies!" Indeed, the Mexicans ran and walked over fallen Texan bodies. Of course, many died on both sides, but all 183 Texans at the fort were killed. Among them were Davy Crockett and Jim Bowie, both famous woodsmen and fighters. Only about 15 people, mostly American women and children, were spared from the massacre. The Alamo fell on March 6, 1836.

However, the Americans, headed by Sam Houston, held a convention. "We are free!" they exclaimed. They declared their independence and established Texas as the "Lone Star Republic," with a flag of its own. They wrote a constitution and elected Houston as commander of the army.

Later, Houston formed a new army and fought Santa Anna and his men, surprising the Mexicans while they were taking their siesta near a river. Shouting, "Remember the Alamo! Remember the Alamo!" the Americans defeated the Mexican army and captured Santa Anna, who signed a treaty giving up Texas. Texas remained a republic until 1845, when it became a part of the United States.

The Southwest. A *boundary* is the dividing line between two states or two countries. Since it's only an imaginary line, it resulted in a conflict between the United States and Mexico with regard to Texas. "This part of land is mine!" Mexico said. "No, this land is mine!" the United States insisted. There was no one to judge the issue; hence, the President of the United States sent an army to Texas. Fighting broke out between soldiers of the two countries. But it didn't last long. The United States won in 1848, receiving, as a result of that war, all of Mexico's claims to territories north of the Rio Grande River. After paying $15,000,000 to Mexico, the United States received land which would become California, Nevada, Utah, New Mexico, parts of Colorado, Wyoming, and a big slice of Arizona. Later, for $2,000,000, the United States bought the rest of Arizona from Mexico.

The Great Gold Rush. In 1848, James Marshall worked at John Sutter's Sawmill in Coloma, California. On June 24, 1848, while working at the mill, he saw shining metal flakes among the rocks! "It's gold! It's gold!" he shouted. News spread throughout the country like wildfire. By 1849, about 100,000 fortune seekers, called the Forty-niners, rushed to the West Coast. These miners found gold all up and down a 150-mile strip of land. The next year, California became a state.

By 1850, there were 31 states and a number of territories.

In 1886, another gold rush began at Fortymile Creek in the Alaskan Yukon.

Today, many reconstructed ghost towns, such as Deadwood Gulch, South Dakota, a gold rush scene in 1876, are just tourist attractions.

The Civil War

As the United States expanded, the differences between the industrialized North and the rural South became apparent.

The northern factories manufactured cloth, guns, and many other things. However, Europeans also manufactured the same products which were cheaper. So some manufacturers urged the government to put tariffs on the imports to protect the American manufacturers.

On the other hand, few large cities existed in the South. Most southerners worked on farms and sold their crops to people in the North and in Europe. There were large southern farms, called *plantations*, where blacks from Africa worked as slaves. The North wanted all people to be free; they didn't like the slavery that existed in the South.

In view of this and other issues—especially states' rights—
the North and the South drifted apart. There were conflicts over
the doctrine of states' rights, trade and tariffs, and slavery. At
this time, Abraham Lincoln was elected as the new president.
But eleven states—South Carolina, Mississippi, Florida, Alabama, Georgia, Louisiana, Texas, Virginia, Arkansas, Tennessee, and North Carolina—seceded from the Union and established their own country, the Confederate States of America,
headed by President Jefferson Davis. At that time, the United
States had 35 states. Missouri and Kentucky didn't leave the
Union. Later, the new state of West Virginia, which separated
from Virginia in 1863 over the issue of slavery, joined the
Union.

The United States before the Civil War

The United States had already 35 states when the Civil War
took place.

Date of Statehood of the First 35 States			
State	*Date*	*State*	*Date*
1. Delaware	1787	18. Louisiana	1812
2. Pennsylvania	1787	19. Indiana	1816
3. New Jersey	1787	20. Mississippi	1817
4. Georgia	1788	21. Illinois	1818
5. Connecticut	1788	22. Alabama	1819
6. Massachusetts	1788	23. Maine	1820
7. Maryland	1788	24. Missouri	1821
8. South Carolina	1788	25. Arkansas	1836
9. New Hampshire	1788	26. Michigan	1837
10. Virginia	1788	27. Florida	1845
11. New York	1788	28. Texas	1845
12. North Carolina	1789	29. Iowa	1846
13. Rhode Island	1790	30. Wisconsin	1848
14. Vermont	1791	31. California	1850
15. Kentucky	1792	32. Minnesota	1858
16. Tennessee	1796	33. Oregon	1859
17. Ohio	1803	34. Kansas	1861
		35. West Virginia	1861

On April 12, 1861, the Civil War broke out when the Confederates fired artillery on Fort Sumter off the coast of Charleston, South Carolina. The opposing sides, the *Federal Union* (the North) and the *Confederacy* (the South) mobilized their armies and navies. On July 21, some 30,000 Union soldiers en route to the Confederate capital of Richmond, Virginia, were stopped at Bull Run (Manassas) and driven back to Washington. This defeat prompted the Union to recruit 500,000 men to serve in the army.

Ready For Action!

In February 1862, General Ulysses S. Grant of the Union Army captured the Confederate strongholds of Fort Henry and Fort Donelson in western Tennessee. That began the first major campaign of the war, which was to result in the death of many soldiers and sailors on both sides.

By March 1865, casualties and desertions plagued the army of Confederate General Robert E. Lee. It was then that General Grant, who was given the title of supreme commander of the Union armies in March 1864, made his final advance at Five Forks and captured the native-burned city of Richmond on April 3, 1865. He accepted Lee's surrender at nearby Appomattox Court House on April 9, 1865. On April 26, Union General William T. Sherman received the surrender of Confederate Lieutenant J. E. Johnston, ending the Civil War. Then the nation became united again.

The Post-Civil War

During the years after the war, the United States continued expansion and industrialization. Many people moved westward, and millions of foreign immigrants arrived and helped to build roads, railways, and industrial plants.

Conclusion

Due to economic and political interests, the United States participated in a number of foreign wars. It declared war on Spain over Cuba; it also fought the Spanish in the Philippines. The Spanish soldiers were in the verge of collapse in the hands of Filipino revolutionaries when the Americans intervened in the war. The Americans won the war and acquired the Philippines from Spain after the Treaty of Paris was signed on December 10, 1898. However, war broke out between the Americans and the Filipinos when an American soldier shot a Filipino soldier on a bridge in the suburbs of Manila. Of course, the Americans defeated the Filipinos. Moreover, the United States also brought into its fold Guam and Puerto Rico. The Philippines received its independence from the United States on July 4, 1946, after World War II.

The United States participated in World War I, World War II, the Korean Conflict, and the Vietnam Conflict. It engaged in a long cold war with the Soviet Union. And, most recently, it led the victorious Allied Forces in the Persian Gulf War that defeated Iraq's Saddam Hussein.

Government **21**

Government is defined as an established system of political administration by which a community, town, city, state, or nation is governed and regulated. A nation without a government would be in chaos; that is why every community or country has some kind of government.

How a government is formed and run is an important segment of a student's life. It is through studying government that your child will know how the citizenry takes part in the administration of government. For instance, by studying government, he'll learn the different types of government and how our national government is different from those of other nations.

(For subject areas studied in Government from kindergarten through grade 6, see pages 214 – 218.)

Types of Government

Generally, governments are identified as *federal, confederate, unitary,* and *totalitarian.*

Federal. The United States is a *federal republic* composed of a national government, fifty state governments, and many local governments. It is different from the governments of other countries of the world. The United States Constitution adopted in 1789 gives certain powers to the national government and reserves all other powers to the states. In other words, while the Federal Government promulgates national laws and policies, state governments pass and implement laws for the benefit of their local people.

Confederate. A *confederate government* gives more power to the individual states and less power to the central government. For instance, during the Revolutionary War, the country had a weak central government which proved inadequate to govern the nation; it was governed by the Articles of Confederation. During the Civil War, the southern states referred to themselves as the *Confederacy,* or the *Confederate States of America.* However, that type of government was changed when the United States Constitution was approved in 1789.

Unitary. In a *unitary government,* the central government is the only government body; it holds all the power in governing all parts of the country. Great Britain's government is a unitary government. Its Parliament is both the *legislative* (lawmaking) and *executive* (law-enforcing) branches of its government. It elects the country's prime minister, who acts like the president of a country. He or she can be dismissed by majority votes of the same body.

Totalitarian Dictatorship. *Totalitarian dictatorship* is the most distinctively modern form of government. In general, a dictatorship is established when anyone in power continues to hold on to his position even if his tenure of office has ended, or when any powerful person seizes by force the reigns of government. Usually, a dictator with the help of the armed forces, tries to change the country's society or tries to prevent the modernization of an existing society. To accomplish his mission, he imposes control over all freedoms—freedom of the press, freedom of speech, and abolishment of all political parties. He also may establish his own secret police and spy network.

The Three Branches of the Federal Government

The United States Constitution divides the national government among three co-equal branches: *executive, legislative,* and *judicial.*

The Executive Branch. The highest executive authority rests with the President. He is the head of state, the commander-in-chief of the Armed Forces, and the nation's treaty maker. He is in charge of enforcing laws. The President is elected by the people through electoral votes every four years. At present, he can only seek office for two consecutive terms.

While he is head of the Armed Forces, he can't declare war, which only Congress can do. However, he can use the Armed Forces in emergencies. If you recall, after President Bush sent troops to Saudi Arabia, Congress met and gave him the authority to use military might if needed in the Persian Gulf. Although it wasn't a declaration of war, it seemed like one, for the United States engaged a war with Iraq, which it won with flying colors.

a. *The Vice President.* The Vice President is elected on the same ticket as the President. He acts as President of the Senate. While he can travel abroad to represent the President in treaties or to attend funerals, he just acts as a guest in ribbon-cutting ceremonies or the like. Of course, if the President is incapacitated or dies, the Vice President takes over the reigns of the government.

b. *Cabinet.* The President is assisted by members of his *Cabinet* who head different governmental departments. Members of the Cabinet are screened and approved by the Senate. At present, there are thirteen departments, each headed by an official called a *Secretary.* They are the Departments of State, Defense, Treasury, Justice, Interior, Labor, Commerce, Agriculture, Housing and Urban Development, Energy, Health and Human Services, Education, and Transportation.

The Legislative Branch. Congress is the legislative branch of the government. It's a two-house legislative body (called *bicameral)* composed of the *lower house* (called *the House of Representatives)* and the *upper house* (called the *Senate).*

The Congress has 435 members in the House of Representatives. They are elected by the people in their districts every two years. The House elects its own head, called the Speaker. Meanwhile, the Senate has 100 members, two senators representing each of the 50 states of the country. They are elected every six years. As already mentioned, the Vice President acts as President of the Senate.

All bills must be passed by both houses of Congress before they are forwarded to the President for approval. In particular, revenue bills originate in the House of Representatives.

Congress also has the power to say to the President, "That's enough! You're fired!" As you can see, by a majority vote of Congress, the legislative branch of the government can dismiss (called *impeach)* a President of this country. No President has yet been impeached by Congress. President Richard Nixon, due to the Watergate scandal, was placed in a very difficult situation. His words in response to the well-publicized investigation could be summed up in a few words, "I've had enough! I resign!"

The Judicial Branch. The judicial branch is composed of courts, the highest of which is the Supreme Court, a nine-member body appointed by the President. It has the power to review and invalidate any legislative, executive, and administrative acts that are against the provisions of the Constitution. It is also called the *Court of Last Resort* in appeals from lower court decisions. In other words, important cases are brought from the lower courts to the highest courts for review and ruling. However, all cases not deemed important are referred back, without being acted upon, to the lower courts where the cases were earlier decided.

While the Supreme Court is the highest court in the country, there are a number of other federal courts. Among them are district courts, tax courts, and military courts.

Each state has the power to establish its own court system. For instance, in the majority of states, the highest court is also called the Supreme Court. (In Maryland, the highest court is called the Court of Appeals.) The state Supreme Court acts like the Supreme Court of the United States. While the United States Supreme Court was created by the Constitution, all lower courts were established by Congress.

The three branches of government have equal powers. They operate under a system of checks and balances.

All laws passed by Congress must be approved by the President, unless passed by Congress after a Presidential veto. For instance, President Bush or any future President can say, "No! This is not good. I don't like it. It could only benefit a few segments of society." In other words, the President can veto or reject any proposed laws passed by both houses of Congress if he thinks such laws are not good or are against the Constitution. Congress, however, can answer in some instances, "Yes, we can read your lips, but you're wrong! This proposed law is according to the Constitution. It can benefit the whole country; therefore, this bill is passed into law." In other words, by a vote of two-thirds of its membership, Congress can overrule the President and pass a law.

On the other hand, the Supreme Court can rebuff the President and say, "You erred! Your action on this law violates the Constitution." As you can see, the highest court of the land interprets and decides on the constitutionality of administrative acts or laws to protect the citizens from being victimized by a corrupt government.

The President appoints all nine members of the Supreme Court. Eight of them are called *associate justices* and one is called the *chief justice.* The complete background of any nominee is reviewed by the Senate. The Senate can say, "This appointment is not approved. Recommend another!" Do you remember a Supreme Court nominee rejected by the Senate?

Also, all appointments to the Cabinet undergo the same procedure. Do you remember a Cabinet nominee rejected by the Senate?

The State Government

In the United States, Australia, and Switzerland, state governments have governmental rights or powers under a federal union constitution. In the Federal Republic of Germany and in Canada, the powers of both levels of government are covered by specific constitutional provisions. In Canada, the states are called *provinces.*

Each of the fifty states of the United States has its own constitution. But provisions of such a constitution and other state laws, rights, or regulations must conform with the provisions of the United States Constitution.

Like the Federal Government, states can levy taxes to raise funds for its operations and other purposes, such as aids to education or health-care programs.

State governments are patterned after the Federal Government. They have the *Executive Branch* (the Governor), the *Legislative Branch* (the Legislature, also composed of the House of Representatives or the House of Delegates and the Senate), and the *Judicial Branch* (the Supreme Court). All states, except Nebraska, have both the House of Representatives and the Senate. The majority of states call their legislative branch the *Legislature,* but other call theirs the *Legislative Assembly,* the *General Assembly,* or the *General Court.*

The Executive Branch. The Governor heads the *Executive Branch.* He is elected by a majority vote of the people in the state every four years. The next position to the Governor is the Lieutenant Governor, who acts as the Governor in case the Governor dies, is killed, or is dismissed by the people of the state, who might say, "Get out of office! You don't serve us well." Yes, through a petition, the people, many of whom had elected him to the position, can dismiss him from office. The petition must be signed by a required number of signatories living in the state.

The Local Governments

Counties. At present, there are over 3,000 subdivisions of state governments, called *counties*. A *county* is composed of a number of townships and cities. A county levies taxes and supervises road building and other services. Although it is not like an organized town or city, it is headed by commissioners elected by the people. The number of commissioners—from three to seven—depends on the size of the county.

In some counties, a board of supervisors rules the government. Still, other counties have their own elected county executives, who act as mayors.

The Legislative Branch. Each state is divided into two sets of legislative districts—one for the *lower house* (the *House of Representatives* or the *House of Delegates* or the *Assembly*) and one for the *upper house (the Senate)*. A speaker heads the lower house, while the Lieutenant Governor heads the upper house. The size of the districts depends on the population. There are more state representatives than state senators. Both houses create standing committees, interim committees, joint committees, and conference committees to discuss bills to be passed. All passed bills must also be forwarded to the Governor for approval. Like the President of the country, the Governor can also veto a proposed law.

The Judicial Branch. The Supreme Court heads the *Judicial Branch*. Like the United States Supreme Court, it can review and make rulings on some decisions made by the lower courts. The state courts are general trial courts, special courts, magistrate courts, and justice-of-the-peace courts.

Mayor-Council Governments. The *Mayor-Council plan* is the type of local government used in many towns or cities. The mayor acts as the *executive* of the city, while the council serves as the *legislative body*.

In some large cities, the so-called *strong mayor plan* is used. That is, the mayor is given a broad power to run the local government with the cooperation of the municipal council which passes resolutions or regulations. Some smaller cities, however, use the so-called *weak mayor plan*. Under this plan, the mayor has limited power and the municipal council runs the local government.

Council-Manager Government. In some cities, they use the *Council-Manager plan*. Under this plan, the people elect the city council, then the council hires a professional manager. His duty is to implement the policies and regulations approved by the council. Of course, the manager can be dismissed anytime if the council thinks he's not doing his job well.

Commission Government. Cities using this type of government elect a board of three to seven commissioners. The board acts as both the *executive* and *legislative* branches of government and selects a head from its own members to serve as the mayor.

Conclusion

As you can see, various types of government work in different ways. But as a whole, excluding the dictatorial government, each type of government runs in such a way that it tries to give the maximum services to the people it is supposed to serve. Without government, there would be no peace and order. Without laws and regulations, there would be rampant violation of human rights. And without government, everyone would be on his or her own, resulting in noncooperation among citizens of a nation or among countries of the world.

Unit VII—Math

**The Way to Teach Math
Counting, Place Value,
and Basic Operations
Word-Problem Solving**

22
The Way to Teach Math

Many people consider mathematics as one of the hardest subjects in school. In fact, some students are considered by many as "good" or "not good" in math. In view of this perception, many students shy away from mathematics, thus depriving themselves of good careers in engineering, computers, and allied fields.

Yet a child can be proficient in mathematics if you, as a parent, will teach him to like this subject. Teaching math should be taught from the very beginning—as soon as your child is ready to go to school. At that time, of course, teaching math may only involve counting and learning how to write the cardinal numbers, 0, 1, 2, 3, 4, 5, 6, 7, 8, and 9. Learning these numbers is the very beginning of math, because these are the only numbers that will play their parts in arithmetic and other branches of mathematics.

The basic rules and principles of arithmetic and algebraic operations should be mastered by your child. It's because they're the very basic foundation of learning to be good in mathematics. That's why you should help the teachers teach math to your child from the very start, not in grade 2 or grade 4, because every process of a math problem is solved step by step. But first, a student must know by memory the symbols, equations, and formulas for every branch of mathematics.

The following symbols used in math are $=$, $-$, $\times$, and $\div$ and refer to addition, subtraction, multiplication, and division, respectively. Parentheses and brackets are also used to indicate multiplication. For example, $(7)(6)$ means 7×6. If a multiplication sign is not needed, the product of x and y is written as xy. Division is sometimes indicated not by a $\div$ but by a bar $(/)$. Example: x divided by y is written x/y or a/b.

Some of the other symbols are as follows:

= means equal to

≠ means not equal to

≡ means identical to

> means greater than

< means less than

$y \sim x$ means approximately equal, or equal in value, but not identical.

| means "when" or "if." Example $a = 10 \mid b = 15$ means "a equals 10 when b equals 15."

An exponent is a small figure placed above and to the right of a symbol.

Example:

$4^3 = 4 \times 4 \times 4.$

$x^3 \, y^3 = xxxyyy.$

Sometimes small figures or letters are used as subscripts, placed below and to the right of a symbol, but they have no value or meaning.   Example: The numbers   1 and 2 in $a_1 + a_2$ merely differentiate a_1 from a_2.

The subject areas covered in math at different grade levels are described below:

I. Subject Areas

★ ★ ★ ★ ★

Kindergarten

In kindergarten, the recognition of numbers is the first thing taught to students. The ten *cardinal numbers* are 0, 1, 2, 3, 4, 5, 6, 7, 8, and 9. Of course, kindergarteners must learn how to write these numbers as they are the base numbers from which all other numbers are formed. Samples of the so-called *ordinal numbers* are *first, third, fifth, tenth*, and *fifteenth*. Teach him how to count at least up to 20.

It will be to your child's advantage if you start to teach him simple addition and subtraction. The fractions to be taught are ¼, ⅓, and ½, the parts of a whole.

Usually, you teach him to solve simple math problems with the use of manipulatives, such as marbles.

With regard to time and measurement, teach him how to distinguish time relationships, such as slower or quicker. Teach him also how to sequence events and how to use the calendar.

In measurement, he should learn the relationships of words, such as short-shorter, tall-taller, smallest-largest.

★ ★ ★ ★ ★

Grade I

At this grade level, teach your child to count up to 100 and continue to learn the ordinal numbers, tenth, thirteenth, fifteenth, and more. Also, he should at this time have mastered skip counting by 2s, 5s, and 10s.

In basic operations, he should already be taught how to do a column addition (with three addends that require no carrying or regrouping. In the whole year, he should know how to add two-digit numbers without carrying.

By this time, he should have already knowledge of the days, weeks, months, and years in the calendar. Likewise, he should able to tell the half-hour and one hour time. At this grade level, he should already be able to recognize and count pennies, nickels, dimes, quarters, half dollars, and dollars.

In measurement, he should be introduced to the study of metrics, such as centimeters and kilograms.

He should be able to use oral and picture problems with the use of manipulatives, such as marbles. In simple word problems, the problem should have only a one-step solution; that is, solve the problem by either of the basic operations—addition, subtraction, multiplication, or division.

★ ★ ★ ★ ★

Grade 2

Teach your child to continue learning how to count at least up to 1,000. By this time, he should be able to use comparison of figures, such as with the use of "more than," "less than," and "equal to" (>, <, =) signs.

By the second grade, let him master the use of cummutative and associative principles. Example of a cummutative principle use in addition and multiplication: $4 + 5 = 5 + 4; (4 + 5) + 7$

= 9 + 7. As you can see in the use of the cummutative principle, the numbers, in whatever arrangements they are, will produce the same answers.

Multiplication is introduced in Grade 2. The use of the cummutative principle is also taught. Example: $3 \times 4 = 4 \times 3$; $(3 \times 4) \times 2 = 8 \times 3$.

By this time, he should continue to identify simple fractions.

Learning how to use the calendar and how to recognize paper currency should be continued at this time.

In the study of measurement, learning the use of standard measurements such as inch, pint, and pound, is a must.

In solving math problems, he should solve simple word problems.

★ ★ ★ ★ ★

Grade 3

At this grade level, your child should have mastered the so-called *place value* up to 999,999; that is, the value of certain numbers in certain places of a group of numbers. For instance, in the numeral 3,450, the number 4 represents 400.

By this time, too, he must already know how to round numbers.

In this grade, he should be able to add and subtract three-digit numbers without carrying or regrouping.

The multiplication by a two-digit number by a two-digit number (23×22) should be mastered in this grade.

In division, two-digit, three-digit, and four-place dividends should be divided by a single-digit divisor. For example, $24 \div 8 = 3$.

With regard to fractions, he should know the different fractions; for instance, fractions with the same denominators and fractions with different denominators.

★ ★ ★ ★ ★

Grades 4, 5, and 6

At these grade levels, your child should have mastered counting, numeration, place value, time, money, measurement, and solving word problems (whether they require one-step, two-step, or three-step solutions).

II. Definition of Math Words

To guide you in teaching math to your child, here are definition of some words:

Addend—Any one of a set of numbers to be added. In the equation $3 + 4 = 7$, the numbers 3 and 4 are *addends*.

Addition—A combination of two or more numbers to get a new number. The numbers to be added are called the addends and the result is called the *sum* of the addends.

Associative principle (also known as **grouping principle**)—An operation in addition or multiplication in which the result is the same, regardless of the way the numbers are grouped.

Example: $4 + (6 + 3) = (4 + 6) + 3$

$3 \times (2 \times 5) = (3 \times 2) \times 5$

Borrow—The term used for regrouping that is involved in subtraction.

Example:

$$
\begin{array}{r}
^{2}\ ^{15} \\
3\ 5 \\
-1\ 7 \\
\hline
1\ 8
\end{array}
$$

Carry—The term used for regrouping that is involved in addition.

Example:

$$
\begin{array}{r}
^{1} \\
61 \\
+19 \\
\hline
80
\end{array}
$$

Congruent angles—Angles that have the same size.

Congruent segments—Segments that have the same size.

Cummutative principle (also known as **order principle.**)—An operation in addition and multiplication in which the order of the addends (or factors) does not affect the sum (or product) when two numbers are added (or multiplied).

Examples: $2 + 7 = 7 + 2$; $3 \times 4 = 4 \times 3$.

Denominator—The number placed below or to the right of the line or a slash in a fraction.

Digits—Any numeral from the base ten system 0, 1, 2, 3, 4, 5, 6, 7, 8, 9.

Division—The process of finding how many times a number (the *divisor*) is contained in another number (the *dividend*). The result is called the *quotient*.

Dividend—The number that is divided by the divisor. In the problem 36 ÷ 8, 36 is the *dividend*.

Example:

$$8\overline{)36} \text{ — dividend}$$

Divisor—The number that is used to divide the dividend to get the quotient. In the problem 36 ÷ 8, 8 is called the *divisor*.

Example:

$$8\overline{)36}$$
divisor

Empty set— A set that has no objects in it.

Equality (equals or =)—The state of being equal or the same. The statement 6 + 4 = 8 + 2 indicates that the number 6 + 4 is exactly the same as 8 + 2.

Equation—A sentence that involves the use of the equality symbol. Examples: 3 + 6 = 9; 5 + □ = 7.

Equivalent fractions—Two fractions that have the same amount of a given object or two fractions that have the same products.

Exponent—A small figure or a symbol placed above or to the right of another symbol to show how many times the latter is to be multiplied. In the symbol 5^4, the 4 indicates that 5 is used as a factor four times. Thus:

$$5^4 = 5 \times 5 \times 5 \times 5 = 20$$

Factors—The numbers that are multiplied. In the equation, 5 × 7 = 35; the 5 and 7 are the *factors* of 35.

Fraction—Any quantity expressed in terms of a numerator and a denominator.

Example: ⅛, ¾, ⅔

Greater than (>)—One of the so-called *inequality relations* indicated by symbols.

Examples: 7 > 5, 18 > 13, 50 > 30.

Grouping principle—(See **associative principle**).

Improper fraction—A fraction that has a numerator that is greater than or equal to the denominator.

$$\frac{12}{4} \qquad \frac{5}{5}$$

Inequality (≠, >, <)—A relation that indicates that two numbers are not equal or the same; one may either be greater or less than the other.

Least common denominator—The least common multiple of the denominators of two or more fractions.

Less than (<)—Any of the two basic inequality relations.

Examples: $3 < 6$; $31 < 37$; $40 < 60$.

Minus (−)—The symbol used to indicate the subtraction operation.

Mixed numeral—The symbol used for a fractional number which is greater than 1 composing a whole number symbol and a fraction symbol.

Examples: 2 ¾, 3 ⅜, 6 ⅔.

Multiplication—The process of finding the number of quantity (known as *product*) acquired by doing repeated additions of a specified number or quantity (*multiplicand*) a specified number of times (as indicated by the *multiplier* .

Example: $3 \times 6 = 18$ or $3 \cdot 6 = 18$ which means $6 + 6 + 6 = 18$.

Multiplicand—The number that is to be multiplied by another (the *multiplier*).

Multiplier—The factor that multiplies or increases.

Numeral—A symbol used to represent a number.

Numerator—Any number indicated by the numeral above a line or a slash in a fraction symbol.

Ordinal number—While a cardinal number (1, 2, 3) refers to a *quantitative* aspect of a set of objects, an *ordinal number* refers to the position of one object in a given set. Examples of ordinal numbers are *first, second, third,* and so on.

Order principle—(See **cummutative principle**).

Parentheses (( ))—The symbols that indicate grouping or order of operations.

Examples: $(6 \times 3) - 3 = 15$; $4 \times (5 - 3) = 8$.

Place holder—A small box in which the solutions to equations are placed.

Example: 5 + 7 = ☐

Place value—The system that involves the writing of numerals for numbers, using a definite number of digits. The placement of a certain number in the order of the numerals represents its value. In the numerals 3546, the 4 represents 4 tens or 40; the numeral 5 represents 5 hundreds or 500; the 3 represents 3 thousands or 3000 (or 3 × 10 × 10 × 10).

Plus (+)—The symbol used to indicate the process of addition.

Example: 5 + 6 = 11 ("5 plus 6 equals 30").

Product—The answer in multiplication.

Quotient—The result or answer in division.

Ray—A point on a line and all the points on one side of that point that are on that line.

Regrouping—The process of *carrying* or *borrowing* in addition and subtraction.

Rounding—The process of giving an estimate or an approximation for a number.

Set—A collection or a group of objects.

Skip Counting—The system of counting by multiples of a given number. Examples: Counting by twos—2, 4, 6, 8, 10.

Subset—Any set within a set.

Whole number—Any number in a set. Examples: (0, 1, 2, 3...10, 12, 15).

Thinking by Steps

The basic principle of all mathematics, from arithmetic to calculus, is "thinking by steps"; that is, solving math problems step by step.

In other words, you're given a certain set of facts (called a *problem*) to find the answer or solution. You get what is asked from what is given. So you have to solve it, one step at a time to find the correct answer.

From the simplest addition to the most complex calculus, each step is built directly on the step that came before it.

For instance, you teach your grade 1 child to add 1 plus 1 before he can add 1 plus 2. Of course, before that, he should learn the cardinal numbers, 0, 1, 2, 3, 4, 5, 6, 7, 8, and 9.

Needless to say, he should master addition before he is taught multiplication. He should master multiplication before he is taught division.

Algebra

Algebra is introduced in the upper elementary grades. It may be defined as a game involving a series of riddles in which a number is hidden.

Here's a simple example of an algebraic operation:

$x = 3 + 8$

In order to find x, your child simply adds 3 plus 8, which is 11. Hence, x is 11.

Of course, the problems or puzzles become harder as they become complex. However, the same rules are applied. In other words, your child needs to learn the first simple steps before he is led to the succeeding steps. In algebra, letters replace unknown or hidden numbers.

Geometry

Geometry is introduced in grade 1. For example, geometrics to be learned at this grade level are square, circle, triangle, rectangle, open figure, closed figure, inside and outside of a figure, point, segment of a line, path of a line, curved line, straight line, same size figure, and shape of figure.

By knowing these things, your grade 1 child will learn how to match cutouts with figures, curves, or segments.

The simplest geometric figures are circle, square, triangle, and rectangle. They may be defined as follows:

Circle: A *circle* is a plane figure bounded by a single curved line, every point of which is equal in distance from the point at the center of the figure.

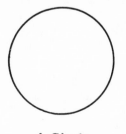

A Circle

Square: A *square* is plane figure with four equal sides and four right angles.

A Square

Triangle: A *triangle* is a figure with three angles and three sides.

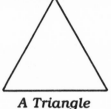

A Triangle

Rectangle: A *rectangle* is any four-sided plane figure with four right angles.

A Rectangle

Other Geometrics. On the other hand, here are examples of a segment and open and closed curves. The figure below is a line segment or a simple segment (A line segment is a subset of the set of points on a line; for instance, the line segment XY is composed of the points X and Y and all the points of that line that are between X and Y.

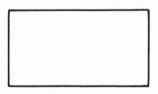

x   *y*

A Line Segment

The figure below is a plane curve. Your child can draw pictures of a plane curve if he moves his pencil or pen continuously along his paper without lifting it from the paper until he is finished doing it.

A Plane Curve

These figures are examples of so-called *closed curves*. As you'll notice, your child forms a closed curve, if he returns his pencil or pen to the point where he started.

Closed Curves

Geometric figures are used in teaching fractions. A fraction is part of a whole. For instance, you divide a square into four parts. A part of the square represents one-fourth of the whole.

23

Counting, Place Value, and Basic Operations

As soon as your child enters kindergarten, he should be able to count from 1 to 20. By the end of the first grade, he should be counting up to 100; by the end of the second grade, up to 1,000. Included in counting procedures is skip counting by 2s, 5s, and 10s. For example, 2, 4, 6, 8...5, 10, 15...and 10, 20, 30....

Counting

Teach him to count by using cumulatives, such as marbles, apples, oranges, etc. Also, teach him how to compare numbers.

When he has become an expert in counting, he should also be an expert in place value. Place value involves writing numerals for numbers, using a definite number of digits. In other words, the placement of a certain number in the order of the numerals represents its value.

Place Value

For instance, in the numerals 6453, the 3 represents three ones, or 3; the 5 represents 5 tens, or 50; the 4 represents 4 hundreds, or 400; and the 6 represents 6 thousands, or 6,000 (or 6 × 10 × 10 × 10).

Example:

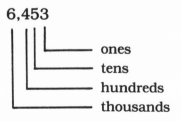

6,453

— ones
— tens
— hundreds
— thousands

Using the so-called *expanded notation* the numerals 6,453 can be rewritten as follows:

6,453 = 6 thousands + 4 hundreds + 5 tens + 3 ones.

Basic Operations

In basic operations, your child should start learning in grade 1 how to add and subtract and how to divide a whole part into small parts, known as *fractions.* With regard to fractions, let him master in this grade the fractions ½, ⅓, and ¼. Make him understand these fractions by showing them in circles, squares, or triangles.

Examples:

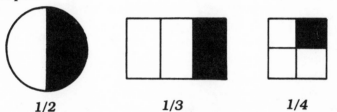

| 1/2 | 1/3 | 1/4 |

In fractions, there are the so-called *improper fractions.* An improper fraction is a fraction that adds up to more than one and should be changed to a whole number and a fraction. For example, ⁹⁄₄ can be changed to a mixed number. (A *mixed number* is the combination of a whole number and a proper fraction.) Thus, the ⁹⁄₄ can be changed to 2 ¼ by dividing 9 by 4.

In grades 1 and 2, simple addition and subtraction should not involve regrouping or carrying or borrowing.

Examples:

$$\begin{array}{r} 33 \\ + \ 16 \\ \hline 49 \end{array} \qquad \begin{array}{r} 29 \\ - \ 18 \\ \hline 11 \end{array}$$

By the third grade, your child should be able to include multiplication in basic operations. So let him memorize the multiplication tables. Also in this grade, he should have mastered comparing fractions by means of the symbols > (more than), < (less than), and = (equal).

At this grade level, he should be able to do regrouping (carrying and borrowing) in basic operations. Also, he needs to begin simple division.

By the fourth grade, he should already have mastered regrouping, addition, subtraction, and multiplication, as well as fractions as part of a whole and as part of a set.

By the end of the sixth grade, he should have mastered the basic operations of fractions.

In the intermediate grades, basic algebra is taught in many elementary schools. Some call it pre-algebra.

Variables

In mathematics, a *variable* is any symbol (y, x, b, c) that can be replaced by a number in order to solve an equation or a problem.

Examples: $4 \times 3 = y$

y must be 12 for this open sentence to be true.

$x = 16 - 7$

x must be 9

These variables are used in addition, subtraction, multiplication, and division. Now we shall discuss the addition of variables.

The Addition of Variables

Commutative Property of Addition. As defined in chapter 22, *cummutative principle* is an operation in addition and multiplication in which the order of the addends (or factors) does not affect the sum (or product) when two numbers are added (or multiplied).

Examples: $12 + 4 = 4 + 12$

$12 + x = x + 12$

Associative Property of Addition. *Associative principle*, known as *grouping principle* is an operation in addition or multiplication in which the result is the same, regardless of the way the numbers are grouped. Parentheses (( )) are used to show which numbers are added first or last.

Examples: $(6 + 5) + 7 = 6 + (5 + 7)$

$(5 + x) + 4 = 5 + (x + 4)$

Additive Identity of Addition. Any number plus (+) 0 is always that number.

Example: $7 + 0 = 7$

Subtraction of Variables

Subtraction in mathematics is the opposite of addition. Therefore, any addition equation can be rewritten as a subtraction equation.

Examples: $4 + 7 = 11$ $7 = 11 - 4$
or
$4 = 11 - 7$

$x + y = z$ $x = z - y$
or
$y = z - x$

Multiplication of Variables

Cummutative Property of Multiplication. Regardless of the way the numbers are multiplied, the product is the same.

Examples: $2 \times 5 = 5 \times 2$
$10 \times 20 \times 5 = 5 \times 20 \times 10$

Associative Property of Multiplication. Regardless of the way the numbers are grouped, the production is the same.

Examples: $4 \times 7 \times 5 = 4 \times (7 \times 5)$
$4 \times 7 \times 5 = (4 \times 7) \times 5$

Multiplicative Identity Property. Any number or variable multiplied by 1 equals the same number or variable.

Examples: $3 \times 1 = 3$
$1 \times y = y$

Division of Variables

Division in mathematics is the opposite of multiplication. Therefore, any multiplication equation can be rewritten as a division equation.

Examples: $5 \times 8 = 40$ $8 = 40 \div 5$
or
$5 = 40 \div 8$

$3b = 100$ $b = \dfrac{100}{3}$
or

$3 = \dfrac{100}{b}$

Time, Money, and Measurement 24

Time, money, and measurement play important parts in our lives. For this reason, students are taught skills to be proficient in handling time and money and to be knowledgeable in measurement.

Subject Areas

★ ★ ★ ★ ★

Kindergarten

In kindergarten, you should teach your child time relationships such as slow-slower, yesterday-today, this week-next week. In other words, he should know how to sequence events.

In measurement, your child should learn comparing, sorting, and ordering. For instance, he should be taught the meaning of words of measurement, such light-heavy, short-tall, near-far, or nearer-nearest.

The use of the calendar is introduced in kindergarten.

★ ★ ★ ★ ★

Grade I

At this grade level, the clock is introduced. Teach him the time to the half hour and the time to the hour. The calender is used in teaching the months, holidays, and seasons. For instance, he should start to name the days of the week, the months of the year, and the seasons of spring, summer, fall, and winter. Fall is sometimes called autumn.

By this time, your child should already know how to recognize and count pennies, nickels, dimes, quarters, half dollars, and dollars.

In measurement, the metric system (centimeter, liter, kilogram) and the standard system (inch, cup, pint, quart, pound) are introduced.

Also, your child should already know how to use a ruler in measuring things; for instance, a pencil maybe four inches in length.

Grade II

Recognition of time relationships and the use of the calender are continued to be taught at this grade level. Also, your child should already know what the the clock's long hand and the short hand represent. In Grade I, he learned the time to the half hour and the time to the hour. Now, he should learn the time to the minute, and the time in the multiples of five.

He should already have skills in mixed counting of money; for instance, from smallest to largest or from largest to smallest.

In measurement, he should continue studying how to measure in (metrics) centimeter, meter, liter, kilogram, or gram. He should also know how to measure in (standard) inch, foot, cup, pint, gallon, quart, or pound.

By this time, he should already know how to measure around shapes; for instance, knowing the distance around each shape.

In the case of liquid measurements, he should know that 2 cups = 1 pint; 2 pints = 1 quart; 4 cups = 1 quart.

The study of temperature, such as using degrees Fahrenheit or degrees Celsius, is introduced in the second grade.

★ ★ ★ ★ ★

Grade III

Teaching the use of the calendar, as well as time and multiples of 5, is continued in Grade III. By now, your child should already be proficient in recognizing and telling the time before the hour, (example, 9:45 or quarter before 10) or the time after the hour (example, 11:15 or quarter past 11).

With regard to money, he should know how to make change from 25 cents, 50 cents, $1.00, $5.00, $10.00, and $20.00.

He should already be knowledgeable in the metric and standard systems of measurement. He should already know how to change metric measures into standard measures and vice versa.

By the end of the third grade, he should be aware of any holiday that takes place in a given month. Also, he should know what a month is known for; for instance, September is usually the back-to-school month.

By this time, too, he should be able to give the ordinal number of the month; for example, the first, the second, and so on.

Regarding seasons, he should be able to know that fall is the time when leaves fall; winter is the time when snow comes and roads become slippery; spring is the time when rains fall and flowers bloom; summer is the time to go on picnics and enjoy other leisure activities.

★ ★ ★ ★ ★

Grades 4, 5, and 6

From Grades 4 through 6, your child should already be a master in skills studied from Kindergarten through Grade 3. In addition to those skills, he should be proficient in the study of months, holidays, and seasons. For example, he should know how to associate symbols with common holidays, such as Santa Claus for Christmas or a turkey for Thanksgiving Day.

Hone your child's skills in time, money, and measurement, and he'll be good at math and other subjects!

Word-Problem Solving

25

In the first four years of his schooling, your child should have mastered the fundamental skills of addition, subtraction, multiplication, and division.

Picture problems and word problems are taught at the same time in grades 1 and 2. (Picture problems involve figures, things, or pictures while word problems involve not only figures but also words.) As soon as he enters grade 3, he should concentrate on solving word problems. Most of the time, the word problem is presented as a story. Solving such a word problem involves one, two, or more steps, depending on the complexity of the problem.

Clue Words

There are some clue or key words in solving problems. The following paragraphs describe some of them.

Addition. Some clue words in addition are "in all," "all in all," "altogether," "sum," and "total."

Example: Janet collected 138 miniature Coca-Cola bottles. Her brother Ronald collected 121. How many did they collect *in all?*

The steps:
1. Read and understand the problem.
2. Look for clue words.
3. Think what operation to use, whether addition, subtraction, multiplication, or division.
4. Solve the problem.

271

The problem:

$$
\begin{array}{r}
138 \\
+\ 121 \\
\hline
259
\end{array}
$$

The answer: They collected 259 bottles in all.

Subtraction. The clue words in subtraction are "how many more," "how many are left," and "the difference."

Multiplication. Some clue words in multiplication are "how many" and "how much."

Division. Some clue words in division are "how many" and "each." When your child divides on a basic level, he is separating something into equal parts.

A Two-Step Problem

Next, we'll discuss a two-step operation. Here are some procedures needed to solve a problem.

Example: If oranges are sold at two for $.50, how many oranges can be bought for $3.00?

The steps:

1. Let your child read and understand the problem.

2. Know what is given.

3. Know what is asked. (In the above example, "How many oranges will $3.00 buy?")

4. Is there a hidden question in this problem? (In the above example, the answer is yes.)

5. Solve the problem. (How many steps are needed to solve the problem?) In this case, the steps to be taken are:

    a. Find out how many $.50 there are in $3.00.

    b. Find out how many oranges $3.00 can buy if every $.50 buys two oranges.

6. Determine what to use, whether addition, subtraction, multiplication, or division. In step a, he must divide $3.00 by $.50 to get the number of $.50 segments. In step b, he must multiply the answer in step a by 2 (the number of oranges that $.50 can buy).

    a. 6

    b. 6 × 2 = 12 oranges for $3.00

The above problem is a simple one. But whatever a word problem is, no matter how complicated, it involves the same procedures—the step-by-step solution. However, in solving word problems, the procedures should be in order; that is, solve it like going upstairs—step first on the first stair, then the second, the third, and so on. In other words, you can't go from step one to step three in mathematics.

Teach your child that solving word problems may take a one-, two-, three-, or even an eight-step solution. Taking such steps is the key to solving word problems.

Unit VIII
Thinking and
and Study Skills

The Brain: The Seat
  of Thinking
Teach Your Child
  How to Think
Teaching Study
  and Test Skills

The Brain: The Seat of Thinking   26

In this unit, we will be discussing the strategies for developing thinking and study skills. But before we do, it would be wise to study how the brain works, because this is the very instrument that humans use to do thinking, planning, and taking actions.

The brain, the computer of the human body, consists of approximately three pints of moist, greyish-yellow matter and is an amazing, complex mechanism. Though it controls all human activities, it weighs only about three pounds, or half as much as a newborn baby. According to scientists, the brain contains from one hundred billion to one trillion nerve cells; it floats in a liquid that acts as its shock absorber. Serving as the "switchboard" of the whole nervous system, it consists of the *gray matter* (the outer cortex of nerve cells) and the *white matter* (the inner mass of nerve cells). It is divided into different compartments where electrical and chemical activities take place, controlled by its self-made codes or by programs like those for a computer.

The Physical Features of the Brain

The brain is divided into three major parts: the *forebrain* or the *front brain*, the *midbrain* or the *middle brain*, and the *hindbrain* or *rear brain*.

The Forebrain. This section consists mostly of the *cerebrum*, formed by two large hemispheres. In the cerebrum, your memory and intelligence thrive; this is where you think, remember, and decide. The *thalamus* is situated in the middle of the brain, above the brain stem; it sends information from ears, nose, eyes, skin, and tongue to the different parts of the body. The *hypothalamus*, located below the thalamus, acts as the relay manager of the nervous system; it is also involved in emotions.

The thalamus, covered by four neuron clusters known as *basal ganglia*, helps control the body's movements. The *limbic system*, another part of the cerebrum, is overlapped by the basal ganglia; it largely controls emotions and actions and also takes part in learning and the operation of the short-term memory. The *archicortex* (original bark), and the *paleocortex* (new bark) cover most of the forebrain.

Each hemisphere in the cerebrum is divided into the *frontal, occipital, temporal,* and *parietal lobes*. These hemispheres are known as the *left brain* and the *right brain*. If your child is left-handed, his right brain tends to be dominmant; if he's right-handed, his left brain tends to be dominant; some people have mixed dominance.

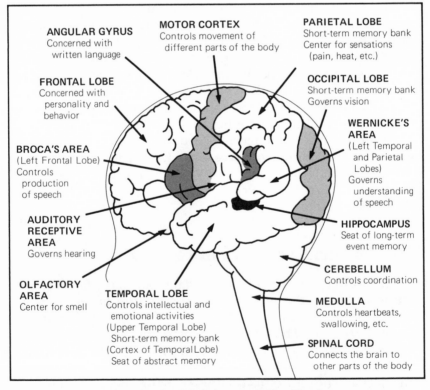

ANGULAR GYRUS
Concerned with
written language

MOTOR CORTEX
Controls movement of
different parts of the body

PARIETAL LOBE
Short-term memory bank
Center for sensations
(pain, heat, etc.)

FRONTAL LOBE
Concerned with
personality and
behavior

OCCIPITAL LOBE
Short-term memory bank
Governs vision

WERNICKE'S
AREA
(Left Temporal
and Parietal
Lobes)
Governs
understanding
of speech

BROCA'S AREA
(Left Frontal Lobe)
Controls
production
of speech

AUDITORY
RECEPTIVE
AREA
Governs hearing

HIPPOCAMPUS
Seat of long-term
event memory

CEREBELLUM
Controls coordination

OLFACTORY
AREA
Center for smell

TEMPORAL LOBE
Controls intellectual and
emotional activities
(Upper Temporal Lobe)
Short-term memory bank
(Cortex of Temporal Lobe)
Seat of abstract memory

MEDULLA
Controls heartbeats,
swallowing, etc.

SPINAL CORD
Connects the brain to
other parts of the body

The Main Divisions of the Brain

According to scientists, the left brain governs logical, mathematical, verbal, and written language skills. The right brain controls imagination, spatial and color sensitivity, and emotions. These are generalities; however, many people possess some of these traits on both sides of the brain.

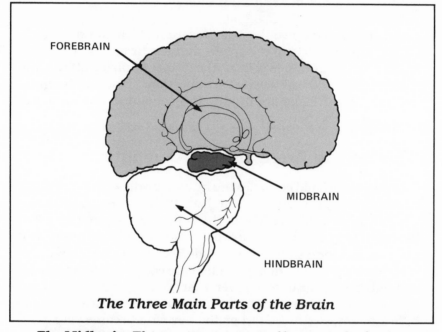

FOREBRAIN

MIDBRAIN

HINDBRAIN

The Three Main Parts of the Brain

The Midbrain. This portion is situated between the forebrain and the hindbrain on top of a network of nerve threads and a nuclei called the *brain stem*, which connects the brain to the spinal cord. The midbrain is the relay station for sensory impulses.

The Hindbrain. This portion forms part of the *pons* and the *medulla*, the brain stem's two lowest communications network stations. These two structures transmit vital messages to and from the spinal cord. Another part, the *cerebellum*, is the largest structure in the hindbrain and the second largest region of the whole brain; it coordinates the body's complex movements.

As you can see, the brain is loaded. It has all the standard equipment, plus all the options. It has power, acceleration, and speed; its capacity ls limitless. I've been loading my brain with data since I was born, but I cannot fill it. I can't empty it, either. Amazing!

The Brain-Mind Connection

What is the difference between the brain and the mind? The brain is matter: it can be weighed, dissected, and examined. But how about the mind? Is it spirit? energy? No one knows. It's not flesh; it's not bone; it's a mystery!

Scientists can't give the exact location of the mind—I can't, either. They are trying to explain that the brain and the mind operate by separate sets of laws; the former by physical laws, the latter by laws still unknown. They speculate that our thoughts, feelings, and dreams are produced by chemical and electrical impulses in the networks of nerve cells.

The Human Brain and the Computer

Maybe we should compare the human brain with the computer. Both contain wirings: the human brain is wired by intricately laid-out nerve fibers; the computer is wired by metal threads. They are both word processors, and both have two kinds of memory: *short term* and *long term.* Your brain's short-term memory keeps track of immediate concerns; for instance, remembering your date at seven that evening or where you put your eyeglasses. Long-term memory stores memories of playing hide-and-seek with the girl or the boy who became your playmate in adulthood.

The computer also has *short-term* and *long-term memory,* called *RAM* and *ROM. RAM stands for random access memory;* the central processing unit (CPU), the brains of the computer, can add to or take from this memory at any time. When a CPU adds information to memory, the process is called *writing;* when information is taken out, it is called *reading.*

ROM stands for *read-only memory.* Although the CPU has access to ROM, ROM cannot be changed: it was "born" with the computer because the manufacturer placed it there. According to an expert on computers, ROM is like a phonograph record because the information is stored permanently, as in long-term memory, while RAM is like a cassette tape on which you can add, delete, or retrieve information, as in short-term memory.

The brain and the computer are alike; it is said that the computer is patterned after the human brain.

Input and Output. When you put information into your brain or into your computer, the information is called *input;* when you retrieve information, it is called *output.* It's like depositing and withdrawing money at the bank; without a deposit, you can't make a withdrawal. The same is true with the computer. The human brain, however, has feelings. The computer doesn't; it can't fall in and out of love. A human being writes the computer's program, but the brain writes its own program. The computer is controled by "on" and "off" signals, but the brain is always "on"—unless the owner is dead.

In a way, the brain and the mind may be similar to the computer and the software: the brain is the computer and the mind is the software. Without the mind, the brain can't function; without the brain, the mind can't function. They are the two-member team that drives your body.

How Does the Brain Work?

Types of Cells. According to scientists, the brain is governed by two types of cells: *glial* or *neuroglial cells* and nerve cells called *neurons.* The former do much of the basic biochemical work, while the latter perform the brain's main work of processing impulses from sense organs.

Neuroglial Cells. The neuroglial cells help and nourish the neurons. They keep the neurons separated by "gluing" them so that the messages in one neuron do not interfere with those in another. They are the brain's welders.

The Neurons. Each neuron has three main parts: the *cell body,* the *axon,* and the *dendrite.* The cell body is a central nucleus composed of a sticky fluid containing microscopic structures; the axon is a slim "tree trunk" that transmits signals between the cell body and other cells and between other parts of the body and the brain through stations known as *synapses.* The dendrite is a short fiber cable that relays signals to its own cell body. Each neuron receives and transmits information signals through thousands of tiny nerve wires that join it with other neurons in the nervous system. The neurons are divided into different groups, each with its own neurotransmitter.

Neurotransmitters are brain chemicals that control the flow of messages through synapses over which the messages jump from the axons to waiting dendrites. These are called "handshakes" between neurons. Millions of handshakes make up a single response, thought, or memory. This activity takes place in the cortex, the outer layer of the brain. Here the neurons process the complex stream of information flowing from the sense organs. After being processed, these electrical and chemical messages are relayed by neurons to deeper layers of the cortex, to other brain structures, and to other parts of the body.

Floyd Bloom, a neuroanatomist at the Scripps Clinic in La Jolla, California, believes that perception, memory, and self-awareness become scrambled when brain chemistry goes awry. Once when I was printing out the manuscript of one of my books, the printer produced strings of letters like xuelghcwptndkaaqklc. Probably the electrical activity between the computer, the software, and the printer got scrambled. The computer, like the mind, goes crazy too.

How Information Is Processed

According to one theory, input from the senses to the brain first enters the short-term memory, where information is stored as coded sounds of words. New items entering the short-term memory drive out the old ones, as if saying "Get out of here!" When items are repeated again and again in a process called *rehearsal,* their stay is prolonged, and the rehearsed and remembered items move to the long-term memory bank.

Kinds of Long-Term Memory. Scientists divide long term memory into *stimulus-response memory, event memory,* and *abstract memory.* Stimulus-response memory makes you salivate when you hear someone say "Let's eat now!" Event memory may help you remember your childhood, even if you're already in your eighties. Abstract memory has a huge capacity; it stores general knowledge and the meanings of objects and events. It is located in the neocortex, the brain's outer gray layer. Some scientists believe that memory formation involves creating chains of molecules called *peptides*—possibly one for each memory created. These peptides are the brain's microchips.

Data Retrieval System. If you're using a computer and want to store names and addresses, you use codes for input and output. For instance, you may create codes with the first three letters of the last name and the last two numbers of the address, and then save them. To retrieve the same data with another program, you key in the same letters and numbers.

You do the same thing with the brain. You code your ideas by forming codes or key words, and then your brain stores them. I call this process *coding*. You retrieve this information from your long-term memory by using the same codes or key words to help you find and obtain the data. I call this process *decoding*.

How Data Is Stored

The brain automatically saves information after a number of repetitions. You don't have to save it by hitting the special control keys as you do on the computer. When I want to place data in my brain, I don't say "save"; the information is saved automatically by my body's computer. The trouble is that I can't delete any information. The more I try to delete, the more I save. In spite of that, I like my brain; it doesn't say "Disk is full!"

Now that we already know how the brain works, let's go to the next chapter on how you can teach your child to use his brain; that is, to learn how to think.

Teach Your Child How to Think   **27**

The term "think" covers a wide range of mental operations. According to the dictionary, "think" is the general word meaning to exercise the mental faculties to form ideas and use them for decisions and actions. It may also mean to do the internal processing of external responses received by an individual through the senses: *seeing, hearing, smelling, tasting,* and *feeling.*

Needless to say, your child should learn how to think, even at an early age, if you want him to be able to succeed in school and in life. He needs "thinking skills" in subjects such as reading, math, science, and history.

In reality, teaching a child to develop thinking skills is a complex procedure. In fact, thinking experts and school teachers use different approaches to teaching children how to think. There are major thinking skills and subskills, and some of them overlap each other.

Basic Thought Groups

Most authors agree that in thinking, the following five basic thought groups are used:
1. Input
2. Retrieval
3. Processing
4. Output
5. Decision and action

I. **Input:** *Data Gathering.* The gathering of information to be stored in the brain involves the senses: seeing, hearing, smelling, tasting, and feeling, which, of course, are accomplished by the eyes, ears, nose, tongue, and skin. (See *The Senses,* pages 133-135.)

To help your child use this process, ask him some questions such as:

Seeing: "What is the man doing?"
Hearing: "What is your friend saying?"
Smelling: "How does the fruit smell?"
Tasting: "How does the mango taste?"
Feeling: "Are you cold?"

II. **Retrieval:** *Recall of information stored in the short- or long-term memory.* You may provide statements and questions to help your child draw ideas, inferences, or conclusions from the facts, feelings, responses, or experiences acquired in the past and imbedded in the short- or long-term memory. (See *Short- and Long-Term Memory,* page 280.)

In order for your child to retrieve facts or information from his short- or long-term memory, he should be able to participate in some activities, such as:

naming	identifying	recalling
describing	listing	

Here are some questions/statements that may lead to "retrieval":

Naming: "What are the New England states?"
Listing: "List the things you'll bring to class."
Describing: "Describe what happened in the meeting."

III. **Processing:** *Organizing or grouping of facts and information gathered from the short- or long-term memory.* The evaluation should be based on processes such as:

summarizing	categorizing	classifying
sequencing	sorting	synthesizing
finding cause-and-effect relationships	analogy making	relating

Another Type of 'Processing'

(Also see *Sciences Processes*, pages 135—136.)

Examples:

Summarizing: "Can you summarize the first chapter of the book?"

Classifying: "What are the seven classification groups of plants and animals?"

Sequencing: "Please arrange the numbers in sequence."

Again, the senses play major parts in drawing the above processes from the information stored in your child's biocomputer. To attain them, you have to make some statements or ask some questions that may lead to the above processes.

IV. **Output:** *The evaluation of facts: for instance, the explanation or giving of reasons for the cause of any results of an observation or an experimentation based on available information.* To help your child get results from evaluation, he should apply some of the following processes:

evaluating	speculating	Investigating
generalizing	contrasting	

Examples:

Speculating: "Can you speculate what the hero will do in the next chapter?"

Evaluating: "Evaluate the solution to the problem based on the given facts."

Generalizing: "What are the characteristics of amphibians?"

V. **Decision and Action:**   *The making of a decision and taking of an action based on an individual's evaluation of given facts.*

Examples of skills needed in conclusion are:

inferring   Interpreting

Examples:

Inferring: "What evidence can you cite that proves that he has made the wrong decision?"

Interpreting: "Give your own opinion on what he said."

A conclusion may be made based on different situations. For instance, when your child has already evaluated the problem or the current situation, he has to conclude what the solution is or what action should be taken. Then he must decide and act!

Decide and Act!

For example, when your child is trying to solve a math word problem, he must take the following steps:

1. Do the data gathering (the known facts and what the problem is or what is to be solved).

2. Name or identify the facts and know the formula to be used or steps to be taken to know the "unknown."

3. Sequence the steps to be taken based on past experiences in solving math problems.

4. Make the judgment whether they are really the steps to be taken and then act to solve the problem.

These thinking processes may also be used in other subjects, such as reading comprehension, science experiments, and historical analysis. However, they may be done in different procedures.

Complex Categories of Thinking

Authors mention different categories of thinking. Some of the most known and important kinds of thinking are as follows:

1. critical thinking
2. creative thinking
3. deductive thinking
4. inductive thinking

It's hard to define the functions of "thinking" processes because sometimes they overlap each other. But we'll try to define each of them simply and concisely.

I. **Critical Thinking.** Critical thinking may be defined as critical analysis and evaluation of beliefs on an issue or issues and the actions to be taken. Sometimes it may involve various strategies for arguments such as in the case of looking for a few reasons on both sides of a case or an issue. Sometimes it may involve the use of imagination to analyze the facts or details of a given situation. Of course, it may also involve speculation of causes or courses of action.

In the elementary school, some of the usual "critical thinking" skills that are taught are as follows:

1. **Recognition and Recalling.** These are the processes of naming, matching, sorting, ordering, connecting, or relating things or events. For instance, you may teach your child to name things: name the things inside the house; match the two sets of balls; put the numbers in order, etc.

2. **Distinguishing and Visualizing.** These are the processes by which a child may solve problems in more systematic and correct ways. That is, he must distinguish the things or the events in certain situations, and he must learn how to visualize the correct procedures to help solve the problem.

3. **Classifying.** This is the process by which objects, living things, and nonliving things are grouped together into certain classes, according to their similarities and differences in sizes, shapes, and colors.

4. **Sequencing and Predicting.** These are the processes by which objects, things, and events are arranged in sequence. They also involve the predicting of what may happen based on the results of observations and inferences.

5. **Analyzing.** This is the process by which a child breaks up a whole into its small parts or steps to find the solution of a problem or learn its important features. For instance, your child may determine the main ideas and the sub-ideas. By analyzing the parts of a theory, a story or a math problem, your child may understand the whole when he breaks it into small parts or steps to find the solution of a problem.

6. **Evaluating:** It is the process of forming an opinion on certain cases, issues, or situations to know whether the steps to be taken are the right ones.

7. **Inferring and Drawing Conclusion:** This is the process by which a child explains his observations of certain things or events and makes his conclusions about them based on what he has observed, studied, and learned.

II. **Creative Thinking.** This skill involves the creation of a complex product; for instance, a story, a machine, or a theory. One of the skills involved in creative thinking is *synthesizing,* which is the process by which your child may combine ideas from available sources or different ways to create new ideas or products. For instance, he may develop a new product based on existing products.

The functions of *critical thinking* and *creative thinking* overlap each other. For instance, critical thinking gets ideas through creative thinking, while there are also instances when creative thinking needs ideas from critical thinking to create a product.

Critical thinking and creative thinking are different in the sense that while critical thinking involves a critical assessment of a belief or an action, creative thinking involves the creation of a product. Both of these skills, however, require new facts or details to be analyzed and used.

III. **Deductive Thinking.** This skill involves the presenting of the generalization to a group; for instance, to support data, cases, or evidence. It also involves seeking additional data.

IV. **Inductive Thinking.** This skill involves the collection, organization, examination of data and the identification of common or general elements. The purpose, of course, is to check the data to see if the "generalization" stands.

In general, deductive (from the general to the specific) and inductive (from the specific to the general) are the two types of inference in drawing conclusions. (See page 82.)

Develop these skills and subskills in your child, and he'll grow up knowing how to accumulate knowledge and using it to be a success in school.

Show him how, and he'll make it!

Teaching Study and Test Skills   28

Learning study skills is one of the most important keys to being a success in school. Without knowing how to study, a child will have a hard time comprehending and digesting facts and information from reading materials, such as books. This is why you should supplement the school's teaching of these skills to your child.

★ ★ ★ ★ ★

I. Kindergarten—Grade 1

In kindergarten and grade 1, your child should have *good habits* at both home and school. Likewise, he should develop his skills in *paying attention, researching,* and *remembering.*

Having Good Habits

To have good habits, be sure that you provide your child with a good diet, plenty of sleep and exercise, and good advice concerning safety rules. For instance, skipping breakfast is not a good habit; it deprives your child of the necessary nutrients needed by his body and brain to function well for the day's activities.

He should also be taught the habit of studying every day, if possible at the same time.

Paying Attention

To learn how to grasp the ideas that you or his teacher wants to convey to your child, you should help him develop the ability to pay attention to what he is being told to do or what he's being told about. To develop this skill, he should listen through his eyes, ears, and mind: his eyes watch yours or the teacher's body language, his ears serve as the microphone, and his mind absorbs and digests what you or his teacher is being talked about.

Watch the Teacher's Body Language

He should also be taught how to pay attention to what he's doing, whether it's drawing, writing, or reading.

Researching

(Review *Teaching Library and Research Skills*, pages 126-130.)

Remembering

In teaching how to remember, you should develop your child's skill in observation: what he sees, what he hears, what he smells, what he tastes, or what he feels. For instance, if he sees words more often, they'll be embedded in his memory, and he'll always remember them. The same is true when he tastes or feels something.

★ ★ ★ ★ ★

II. Grades 2 and 3

At these grade levels, your child should have skills in *getting organized, following directions, researching,* and *taking tests.*

Getting Organized

To develop his skill in organization, you should teach him to have a regular place of study where he'll have all the necessary tools for studying. For instance, he should have his books placed in shelves on or near his study table from where he can easily get them when he needs them.

In going to school, his books, notebooks, pencils, and other supplies should have their appropriate places in his school bag.

Following Directions

Some direction words are as follows:

bring	write	draw	color	circle
close	find	put	name	read

In Grades 2 and 3, your child should already know how to get the main idea or sub-ideas from a short story or an article. The main idea is the most important part of a paragraph or a story. Usually, you'll find it when you ask the questions *who* and *what* or what is the story about? About a bird cage? About a picnic area?

Researching

(Review *Teaching Library and Research Skills*, pages 126-130.)

Taking Tests

To learn how to take tests, teach your child the habit of knowing when the test will be and what the subject matter will be. Then let him review his books. In reviewing, encourage him to make an outline of the subject matter: major topic, subtopic, and supporting details. In addition, you encourage him to review with a classmate, asking each other questions about the subject being reviewed.

Teach him the habit of writing legibly as much as possible, especially in math test, and putting each number in the proper column or alignment, particularly in addition or subtraction.

It is very important to coach your child to pay attention to the *direction words;* that is, what he is supposed to do, whether to circle or underline a letter or words, or fill in the blanks.

★　★　★　★　★

III. Grade 4

By grade 4, your child should have mastered the study skills taught from kindergarten through Grade 3. The skills needed to be honed in Grade 4 are in *reading and writing, organizing information, researching,* and *taking tests.*

Reading and Writing

In grade 4, your child should improve his skills in reading and writing. (Review chapters *Perceptual Skills and Word Analysis,* pages 67-79; *Reading Comprehension,* pages 80-85; *Grammar and World Analysis,* pages 89-104; and *Hone Your Child's Writing Skills,* pages 105-125.)

Organizing Information

To organize information, one must know how to condense. Condensing involves such processes as *outlining, summarizing,* and *diagramming,* or *mapping.*

To master the skill of outlining, your child should be taught how to take notes. While listening to his teacher, he should be able to take notes of the important things that the teacher is talking about: the main idea, the sub-ideas, and the details.

To master the contents of a chapter, a story, or a book, he should be able to know how to make an outline, a summary, and a diagram, which sometimes is called a map.

Outlining. Outlining is the breaking down of ideas in sequence. For instance, the standard outline form uses Roman numerals (I, II, III, etc.), capital letters (A, B, C, D), Arabic numerals (1, 2, 3, 4), and lowercase letters (a, b, c, d).

Here's an example of an outline:

I. First major topic

A. First subtopic of I
   1. First subtopic of A
      a. First subtopic of 1
      b. Second subtopic of 1

   2. Second subtopic of A
      a. First subtopic of 2
      b. Second subtopic of 2

B. Second subtopic of I
   (and so on)

   II. Second major topic
   (and so on)

Summarizing. Summarizing is the presentation of details not included in outlining. It's the process of condensing by which a story or a report is made into a miniature form that contains the answers to the questions *who, when, where, what, how* and *why.*

Diagramming or Mapping. Diagramming is similar to outlining, but instead of the indented A, B, C, 1, 2, 3, and a, b, c, it makes use of graphs or sketches or any form that will present the organization of text from a book. Diagramming is also called *mapping.*

Researching

(Review *Teaching Library and Research Skills*, pages 126-130.)

Taking Tests

At this grade level, he should have mastered the test taking techniques used in grades 2 and 3.

★ ★ ★ ★ ★

IV. Grades 5 and 6

At these grade levels, the skills taught are in *setting goals*, *reading and writing*, *researching*, and *taking tests*.

Setting Goals

When one sets goals, he makes plans either in his mind or in written form about the necessary steps to take to accomplish what he should do in a particular time frame. When you teach your child how to set goals, let him know that if he doesn't know where he has been and where he is going, he will never reach his destination.

Reading and Writing

In Grades 5 and 6, your child should continue to develop his reading and writing skills. For instance, in studying, he should apply the study system developed by Dr. Francis P. Robinson in 1946. This system is popularly known as the SQ3R and discussed in his book, *Effective Study* (New York: Harper, 1946). The SQ3R method, adopted by many people and even cited in several study skills books, comprises five steps: *survey, question, read, review*, and *recite*.

Survey. To survey is to read the chapter headings and the subheads (usually in bold type), and the introductory and summary paragraphs, and to review the questions, that usually appear at the end of the chapter.

Question. Train your child to ask himself questions about the chapter heading and the main text, seeking answers to how and why. He should also be asking himself about what the subject matter is all about.

Read. To read is to grasp ideas and thoughts from the printed page or from hand-scribbled notes to find answers to questions, going from one section to another.

Review. To review is to close the book or the notes and to answer the questions he asked himself, resulting in a general review of the whole assignment. Once in a while, he must open the book or the notes to see what has been learned or memorized.

Recite. To recite is to close the book or the notes and the eyes, or to look out the window and recall the items, answering the questions he must have asked himself.

Researching

(Review *Teaching Library and Research Skills*, pages 126-130.)

Taking Tests

Before taking tests, have your child learned how to prepare for tests. For instance, show him how to organize his notes, including outlining or summarizing. Have him review small chunks of information, remembering a few items at a time.

In a nutshell, study skills and test skills are necessary gauges used to determine what a child is learning or has learned at home or in school. This is why they should be developed in your child at the same time. The mastery of these skills may be reflected in your child's recitation in class and in his grades. In the end, what he has learned will be accumulated in his mind, giving him the tools to cope with school work and his career in the future.

(For more effective studying and test taking strategies, see the book, *Improve Your Grades* (Bookhaus Publishers, P.O. Box 3277, Farmington Hills, MI 48331-2954, $9.95 plus $3.00 postage.)

Bibliography and Recommended Reading

Armstrong, William H. and Willard Lampe II. *Study Tips: How to Study Effectively and Get Better Grades.* Barron's Educational Series, Woodbury, New York.

Bautista, Veltisezar B. *Improve Your Grades: A Practical Guide to Academic Excellence,* second edition. Bookhaus Publishers, Farmington Hills, MI.

Bell, Sandra M. and James I. Wheeler. *Learning Grammar Through Writing.* Educators Publishing Service, Inc., Cambridge, MA.

Berenstain, Stan and Jan. *The Berenstain Bears' Science and Nature Super Treasury.* Bear Facts Library/Random House, New York.

Cangemi, JoAnn, general editor. *Holt Social Studies Regions,* Teacher's Edition. Holt, Rinehart and Winston, Publishers, New York.

Cavandish, Marshall. *The Illustrated Encyclopedia of Plants.* Exeter Books/Simon & Schuster, New York.

Cesinger, Joan. *The Animal Kingdom.* Hayes School Publishing Co., Inc., Wilkinsburg, PA.

Compton, Carol. *Improving Composition through a Sentence Study of Grammar and Usage.* Educators Publishing Service, Inc., Cambridge, MA.

Coulter, Mercie C. (Revised by Howard J. Dittmer.) *The Story of the Plant Kingdom.* University of Chicago Press, Chicago.

Eicholz, Robert E., Phares G. O'Daffer, and Charles R. Fleenor. *Investigating School Mathematics.* Book I, Teacher's Edition. Addison-Wesley Publishing Company, Menlo Park, CA.

Engelmann, Siegfried and Therese. *Give Your Child a Superior Mind.* Cornerstone Library/Simon & Schuster, New York.

Fields, Terri. *Help Your Child Make the Most of School.* Villard Books, New York.

Foltzer, Monica. *Professor Phonics Gives Sound Advice.* St. Ursula Academy, Cincinnati, OH.

Fredericks, Anthony D. *The Reading Comprehension Idea Book.* Scott, Foresman and Company, Glenview, IL.

Fuller, Cheri. *Home Life: Preparing Your Child to Succeed at School.* Honor Books/Harrison House, Tulsa, OK.

Glass, Lilian. *Talk to Win.* Perigee Books/Putnam Publishing Group, New York.

Green, Gordon W. *Getting Straight A's.* Lyle Stuart, Inc., Secaucus, NJ.

Hicks, Laurel Elizabeth. *New World History and Geography.* A Beka Book Publications, Pensacola, FL.

Hohn, Reinhard. *Curiosities of the Plant Kingdom.* Universe Books, New York.

Kline, Morris. *Why Johnny Can't Add.* St. Martin Press, New York.

Loray, Harry and Jerry Lucas. *The Memory Book.* Ballantine Books/Random House, New York.

Maddox, Harry. *How to Study.* Fawcett Premier Books/CBS, New York.

Mammana, Dennis. *Start Exploring Space.* Running Press, Philadelphia, PA.

Moche, Dinah L. *Astronomy Today.* Random House, New York.

Moore, Jo Ellen and Joy Evans. *Learning About Animals.* Evan-Moore Corp., Monterey, CA.

Napp, John L. *Learning About Government.* Media Materials, Inc., Baltimore, MA.

Orton, June Lyday. *A Guide to Teaching Phonics.* Educators Publishing Service, Inc., Cambridge, MA.

Payne, Lucile Vaughan. *The Lively Art of Writing.* New American Library, New York.

Phillips, Wanda . *Easy Grammar.* Isha Enterprises, Scottsdale, AZ.

Rudginsky, Laura Toby and Elizabeth C. Haskell. *How to Teach Spelling.* Educators Publishing Service, Inc., Cambridge, MA.

Sobol, Tom and Harriet. *Your Child in School.* Arbor House/A Quill Edition, New York.

Staple, Michele and Linda Gamlin. *The Random House Book of 1001 Questions and Answers About Animals.* Random House, New York.

Strumpf, Michael and Auriel Douglas. *Painless, Perfect Grammar.* Monarch Press, New York.

Thypin, Marilyn and Lynne Glasner. *A History of the United States.* Entry Publishing Co., New York.

Waddel, Marie L., Robert M. Esch, and Roberta R. Walker. *The Art of Styling Sentences.* Barron's Educational Series, Inc., New York.

Wilder, Lilyan. *Talk Your Way to Success.* Fireside Book/Simon & Schuster, Inc., New York.

Williams, Brian and Brenda. *The Random House Book of 1001 Wonders of Science.* Random House, New York.

Index